EUPHORIA

A Comedy by Mark A. Ridge

ISBN-10: 1539808513
ISBN-13: 978-1539808510

EUPHORIA received its first reading (closed to the public) on July 11, 2009. The reading took place at the Perceptual Motion Dance Studio in Chicago, Illinois. The reading featured the following cast:

JOE MARCH	Michael Wells
GEORGE "TRENT" WILLOWS	Derek Elstro
CORY MORRISON	Andrew Melick
PHIL AHERNE	Thomas Kaefring
AARON LANG	Brian Damson
PATRICK GUNDERSON	Christopher Anton
AGNES PLATT	Deborah Kudla
LORETTA HOLT	Ilene Collins
TINA HOBBS-SHOUSE	Jodi Ewen
GLEN FRUGLEY	Andrew Souders
DONALD GUNDERSON	Mark Collins
ALBERT SUTTON	Bill Boehler
AIMEE RUTH	Bree Gordon
HEATHER HARVEY	Amanda Besinger
FEMALE ONSTAR VOICE	Bree Gordon
MARIE'S VOICE	Alexis Marsh

EUPHORIA received its first workshop reading (open to the public) on October 5th, 2009. The reading took place in the West Studio Theatre in the Raven Theatre Complex in Chicago, IL and featured the following cast:

NARRATOR	Sommer Austin
JOE MARCH	Andrew Pond
GEORGE "TRENT" WILLOWS	Aaron Page
CORY MORRISON	Mark Contorno
PHIL AHERNE	Thomas Kaefring
AARON LANG	Brian Damson
PATRICK GUNDERSON	Andrew Martin
AGNES PLATT	Deborah Kudla
LORETTA HOLT	Ilene Collins
TINA HOBBS-SHOUSE	Tracie Dahlke
GLEN FRUGLEY	Tim Grimes
DONALD GUNDERSON	Fred Uebele
ALBERT SUTTON	Joe Savino
AIMEE RUTH	Bree Gordon
HEATHER HARVEY	Amanda Besinger
FEMALE ONSTAR VOICE	Bree Gordon
MARIE'S VOICE	Amy Wallin
Stage Manager	Amy Nelson
Graphic Design	Bluesoup Design
Sound Recording	Moe Martinez
Director	Andrew Souders

EUPHORIA received an additional workshop reading (open to the public) on November 7 and 8, 2010. The reading took place at Stage 773 in Chicago and featured the following cast:

NARRATOR	Michelle McKenzie-Voigt
JOE MARCH	John Highberger
GEORGE "TRENT" WILLOWS	Aaron Page
CORY MORRISON	Patrick Gannon
PHIL AHERNE	Lee Wichman
AARON LANG	Mark Smaglinski
PATRICK GUNDERSON	Tommy Venuti
AGNES PLATT	Ilene Collins
LORETTA HOLT	Erica Badke
TINA HOBBS-SHOUSE	Traci Nettesheim
GLEN FRUGLEY	Tim Grimes
DONALD GUNDERSON	Marty Grubbs
ALBERT SUTTON	Mark Contorno
AIMEE RUTH	Kelly Schmidt
HEATHER HARVEY	Amanda Besinger
FEMALE ONSTAR VOICE	Erica Badke
MARIE'S VOICE	Amy Wallin
Stage Manager	Hayley Smith-Pilat
Graphic Design	Amy Wallin / Blue Soup
Sound Recording	Moe Martinez
Director	Andrew Souders

The author would like to thank the following individuals for their assistance on this project:

Ashlee Parker, Bob Hughes, Bob Scholl,
Harlan Didrickson, Paige Bailey,
Perceptual Motion Dance Studio,
Stage 773, The Raven Theatre,
and
Amy Wallin as Marie

Synopsis of Scenes

The Play takes place between a Friday Morning and a
Saturday Evening in the following locations:

JOE'S STUDIO APARTMENT
IN AND AROUND AARON'S CAR
A DESERTED GAS STATION PARKING LOT
THE PARKING LOT OF EUPHORIA
THE COMMON ROOM OF EUPHORIA

Cast of Characters

(In Order of Appearance)

JOE MARCH - *A Gay Man Turning 40.*

GEORGE "TRENT" WILLOWS -
A Sexy 23 Year Old Boy Toy with a Brain.

CORY MORRISON – *Joe's Attractive 40 Year Old Neighbor.*

PHIL AHERNE -
A Male Nurse Who Loves Life. 40's. Aaron's Partner.

AARON LANG –
Joe's Best Friend. 40's. A Pharmaceutical Salesman.

PATRICK GUNDERSON -
A Spa Assistant. Good Looking. Early 20's.

AGNES PLATT -
The Spa Trustee. An Ex-Con With A Heart Of Gold.

LORETTA HOLT -
The Beautician Who Is Trying To Quit Smoking.

TINA HOBBS-SHOUSE –
A Young Newlywed in Search of Her Husband.

GLEN FRUGLEY- *A Bi-Sexual Plumbing Fixture Salesman.*

DONALD GUNDERSON-
Ex-Prison Warden /Spa Owner. Patrick's Uncle.

ALBERT SUTTON –
A Single, Politically Incorrect Claims Adjuster.

AIMEE RUTH –
A Butch Lesbian in search of her Feminine Side.

HEATHER HARVEY- *A Single Girl in Search of a Boyfriend.*

ENNIS- *Joe's Cat (Optional)*

OFF STAGE VOICES – *Can Be Pre-Recorded or Double Cast*
FEMALE ONSTAR VOICE, MARIE'S VOICE

"From the start it has been the theatre's business to entertain people . . . it needs no other passport than fun."

Bertolt Brecht

EUPHORIA

A Comedy by Mark A. Ridge

Act One

Scene One

JOE'S studio apartment located in a Chicago North Side Neighborhood. The apartment is sparsely furnished and rather unkempt. Fast food wrappers litter the floor.

It is early morning. JOE and TRENT are asleep under the covers.

The TELEPHONE RINGS and the ANSWERING MACHINE CLICKS on.

JOE. *(On answering machine)* Hi. This is Joe. Sorry I can't take your call. I'm either at work, in the middle of a movie, or I've died of boredom. If it's the first or second, I'll call you back. If it's the third, I probably won't.

The MACHINE BEEPS.

PHIL. *(On answering machine)* Joey, pick up. Joseph, wake up. I know you're there. You better be there. OK, we're on our way over. If you don't answer the door, I'm using our spare key.

JOE tries to wake up. He is extremely hung over, nauseous and surprised to find that he is not alone. He locates his glasses and begins to study the naked body sleeping next to him. As he peeks under the covers, TRENT begins to stir.

TRENT. How you feelin'?

JOE. My mouth tastes like I vomited on a rice cake and then ate it.

TRENT. *(Grabbing the wastebasket)* You need this again?

JOE. No.

TRENT. You want a glass of water?

JOE. No.

TRENT. You want me to rub your shoulders?

JOE. No.

TRENT. *(Picking a bag off the floor)* Hey, there's still a few fries in here.

JOE. Don't eat those.

TRENT. It's no different than eating cold pizza.

JOE. Please don't talk about food. Don't talk about anything. My head is pounding.

TRENT. Don't you like me anymore? Look how flexible I am.

JOE. Please, you're rocking the bed.

TRENT. *(Flexing his arms)* Go on. Feel this. You've got nothing to be shy about. I've seen you hurl.

JOE. Look, this is a little awkward. And please don't take this personally-

TRENT. What? What is it?

JOE. I have no idea who you are.

TRENT. I'm Trent. I hooked up with you guys at Time Out.

JOE. I remember a DJ - and people kept buying rounds. And, I remember this sailor hanging from a pole.

TRENT. *(Saluting)* That was me! My real name is George. Trent is just my stage name. I think George sounds like an accountant.

JOE. What are you, 28, 29?

TRENT. I'm 23.

JOE. God, How did you end up here . . . with me? I'm old.

TRENT. You're not old.

JOE. I'm old and fat and I ate White Castle.

TRENT. You're not fat. I'll bet if you joined a gym -

JOE. I belong to a gym.

TRENT. Oh. How often do you go?

JOE. I belong to a gym. What exactly happened last night?

TRENT. I was dancing and your friend Phil kept giving you money to tip me. Then, we started talking. We talked for over an hour. Then, you started crying.

JOE. God.

TRENT. A lot of people get depressed on their birthdays. So, we hit the drive-thru and I brought you home. Then, you got sick. I gotta take a leak.

> *TRENT grabs his gym bag and walks into the bathroom.*

> *JOE forces himself out of bed. He is still fully clothed in his outfit from last night. He stumbles to the kitchen and grabs some cat food. He almost gags from the smell, but manages to put some into a bowl.*

JOE. Here Kitty. Kitty? Breakfast. *(The cat does not come out. As Joe puts away the food, he is startled by a cockroach.)* DAMMMIT! ROACH. ROACH. ROACH.

> *JOE chases the roach over into the corner and traps it under a cup. The cup slowly moves around the counter.*

> *JOE is totally disgusted. He walks to the center of the room, stomps his foot four distinct times, crosses to the door and unlocks it. Within seconds, the door opens and CORY enters.*

CORY. Where is it?

JOE. On the counter, under that cup. Please throw away that cup. *(Like he has done it a hundred times, CORY gets the roach and starts for the bathroom.)* Oh, wait . . .

It is too late. TRENT comes out dressed in his underwear.

CORY. Oh, I'm sorry.

TRENT. I'm Trent.

CORY. I'm the exterminator.

CORY exits into the bathroom.

TRENT. Kind of early for an exterminator.

JOE. He's my neighbor. We have an agreement. I let him park in my parking space, he takes care of the roaches. He's going to watch my cat while they fumigate the apartment today.

TRENT. He's pretty hot for an older guy.

JOE. Shhh. He's going to hear you.

CORY returns with the litter box.

CORY. I'm taking this now.

JOE. Thanks. *(Embarrassed)* Cory, this is Trent. I mean, George.

CORY. I guess I don't have to ask if you had a good birthday.

TRENT. It was great.

CORY. I heard it all . . . at four o'clock this morning. I'm gonna go finish my coffee and then I'll come back up for the cat. And for the record, Joe is four months older than me.

CORY exits.

JOE. Thanks for putting me to bed and for whatever else you did. But, you don't need to hang around here anymore. You can go. Seriously, it's OK. You should go now. I need to pack.

TRENT. I'm coming with you.

JOE. What?

TRENT. You invited me.

JOE. Look, we may or may not have had a great time last night, I don't remember. But you can't believe anything I said, especially if you were dressed as a sailor. This trip is not for you. You won't have a good time. We never have a good time.

TRENT. Then why are you going?

JOE. It's sort of a tradition . . . just a stupid thing we always do for our birthdays. One of us picks a place and we road trip. It's never fun. Last year, Aaron booked us into this seminar called <u>Communication for Dummies</u>. We didn't speak to each other for three weeks.

TRENT. I told you last night. I can't get into my new apartment 'til the first. I've been sleeping in my car for the last two weeks. I got no place else to go.

JOE. Oh . . . Well . . . I tell you what. . . You can hang out 'til the guys get here. If it's OK with them, then . . .

TRENT. *(Holding up a bag of pot)* Great. I'm all packed.

JOE. You better keep that hidden from Aaron. He'll freak. *(JOE begins to remove his shirt, when he realizes that TRENT is watching him. Embarrassed, he heads into the bathroom.)* I'm gonna take a quick shower. Don't steal anything.

TRENT. Funny.

> *From off stage, the SOUND OF THE SHOWER can be heard.*

> *TRENT does a few early morning stretches. After a moment, he exits into the bathroom to join JOE.*

JOE. *(Off Stage)* I am on the toilet!! Get out of here!

> *TRENT is pushed out of the bathroom.*

> *The INTERCOM BUZZES.*

5

TRENT. You might want to light a match in there. *(Locating the intercom)* Who is it?

PHIL. *(Through the intercom)* Who is this?

TRENT. It's me, Trent.

PHIL. *(Through the intercom)* Trent? Let us up!

> *TRENT opens the front door.*

TRENT. Hello.

AARON. Oh, this is great . . . just great. Does anyone else know you're here?

TRENT. I don't know.

AARON. Where is he?

TRENT. Still in the bathroom. He's kind of slow-moving this morning.

PHIL. I'll bet. Hey, I like those shorts.

AARON. Will you quit staring at him?

PHIL. What exactly happened here last night?

AARON. Phil, that's none of our business.

PHIL. The hell it isn't. Dish.

TRENT. We just talked. He's kind of shy. It took me fifteen minutes to get him out of his shoes.

PHIL. He won't even change clothes at the gym.

TRENT. Then, he threw up on me.

PHIL. Oh, that's hot.

TRENT. He's nice. I don't know why he doesn't have a steady boyfriend.

PHIL. He's way too uptight.

AARON. He just hasn't found the right guy yet.

PHIL. He does have a not-so-secret crush on his downstairs gaybor.

TRENT. I think I just met him. Cute guy. Nice eyes. He came in and killed a bug.

AARON. This is going to ruin everything.

PHIL. Calm down.

TRENT. It was just a bug.

AARON. It's that damn grocery store next door. That's why I hired an exterminator to do the apartment today. It's part of my birthday present to him . . . something sensible.

PHIL. The gift that keeps on killing.

AARON. I said "Part." Hopefully, he'll get the real present on Saturday. Cory is supposed to drive up and surprise Joe for his birthday. He probably won't come now. Just once, I was hoping one of these getaways would work out.

TRENT. Where exactly are we going?

AARON. We?

TRENT. Yeah, Joe invited me.

AARON. *(Yelling)* Joe, you need to get out here.

JOE. *(Yelling from off stage)* George? What are you doing out there?

AARON. George? Who's George?

TRENT. I'm George. Trent is just my stage name.

PHIL. George sounds like an accountant.

JOE. *(Yelling from off stage)* Who are you talking to?

AARON. *(Yelling)* It's just us.

JOE. *(Yelling from off stage)* I'll be out in a minute.

AARON. This doesn't make sense. *(To TRENT)* You're not even his type.

PHIL. Are you kidding? He's everybody's type. What are you doing?

AARON. I'm just trying to tidy up.

PHIL. Hey, are those fries?

7

AARON. Don't eat those. God, you're disgusting.

PHIL. He might be saving those.

AARON. No one saves used hamburger wrappers. No wonder he has bugs.

PHIL. Aaron's a clean freak.

AARON. No, Phil's a slob.

PHIL. I am not.

AARON. His whole family is. You should see his parent's house. It's like a trip to Grey Gardens.

PHIL. It is not.

AARON. It is too.

TRENT. *(To PHIL)* You guys are a couple, right?

AARON. *(After PHIL does not answer)* Yes, we are! Why is this wastebasket just sitting out here? OK, this is too much. Phil, come here. Even you have to admit that this is disgusting.

PHIL. It's vomit. What's the big deal?

AARON. The big deal is . . . the big deal is . . . vomit does not belong in the living room. You are pathetic. Where does he keep his Lysol?

AARON crosses into the kitchen.

PHIL. Are those from Undergear?

TRENT. Oh, I don't remember.

PHIL. Turn around. Let me see the tag.

PHIL checks out the label in TRENT'S underwear.

AARON. Leave him alone.

JOE enters.

PHIL. Happy Birthday. Way to go. Hubba Hubba.

AARON. Joseph, I need to talk to you in private. Now.

TRENT. I'll just hop in there and rinse off. That way you guys can talk about me.

TRENT exits into the bathroom.

AARON. Just put something on before Phil hyperventilates. Why did you just up and leave last night?

PHIL. I think that's pretty obvious.

AARON. Did you really invite him to come with us?

JOE. Well . . .

AARON. What are we supposed to do all weekend with a stupid, little twink? *(To PHIL)* Don't answer that.

JOE. I don't think he's stupid.

AARON. Why are you defending him?

PHIL. 'Cause he's hot.

AARON. You have socks older than he is.

JOE. I'm sorry. You know me. I can't say "No" to people.

PHIL. Our own little Ado Annie

JOE. And, he quoted <u>An Officer and a Gentleman.</u>

AARON. Not Richard Gere again -

JOE. He looked up at me with his big sad eyes and said "I got no where else to go."

AARON. But, this is going to ruin everything.

JOE. I still don't even know where we are going.

PHIL. OK, are you ready? We're going to Euphoria! I got us reservations! Can you believe it?

JOE. I don't even know what that is.

AARON. It's a health spa Phil found on the internet.

PHIL. Yeah, I was in this chat room and Glen69 recommended it. It's just outside of Memphis.

JOE. That's got to be at least an eight hour drive.

9

AARON. Don't look at me. He made all the arrangements.

JOE. Well, I'm not sleeping in a tent again and I'm not peeing in a bush. You know how I am about bugs.

PHIL. The entire North Side knows how you are about bugs.

JOE. I should pack some repellent. *(Starting for the bathroom)* Oh, I better wait.

PHIL. I'll get it! *(Looking for permission)* Can I?

JOE. It's in the medicine cabinet. He won't mind. I think he likes being looked at.

PHIL. It's not him that I'm worried about.

AARON. *(Giving permission)* Go ahead.

PHIL darts off into the bathroom.

JOE. Go on. You're just dying to say something.

AARON. He's just so . . .

JOE. You keep telling me I need to put myself out there.

AARON. Do you realize that while his mother was giving birth to him, we were probably at the movies seeing Flashdance for the fifth time?

JOE. I know he's young . . . but he spent the night. That's an improvement over my last four dates. If I hadn't been so sick -

AARON. You gonna be OK?

JOE. Yeah. Birthdays don't usually get to me, but this one, 40. That's like 280 in gay years.

AARON. My rough one was thirty. I didn't think that perm would ever grow out . . . and remember Phil's mustache?

JOE. I ran into Jeff yesterday. He was with that kid.

AARON. Jeff is an asshole. You should sue his cheating ass. Part of that house should be yours.

JOE. It's not just that. It's everything. It's this dump. It's work. Things between Cory and me don't seem to be happening. I can't get motivated to clean. Look at this dust. You could plant potatoes in here. And to top it off, right now, at this very minute, your boyfriend is in my bathroom watching a go-go boy take a shower.

AARON. *(Yelling)* Phil ! *(To JOE)* I tell you what, next Saturday I'll bring over my <u>No No Nanette CD </u>and we can clean this place from top to bottom. *(Yelling into the bathroom)* What are you doing in there?

TRENT. *(Off Stage)* I'm taking a shower.

AARON. *(Yelling)* Not you.

PHIL. *(Off Stage)* I'm watching Trent take a shower.

AARON *(Yelling)* Enough. Out here, now!

JOE. You don't get it. You've got Phil.

AARON. You wanted Phil?

JOE. No. But, I want to be in a relationship, a real one, one like in the movies. I want my own Debra Winger moment. When Richard Gere walks into that factory and he picks her up and he's all dressed in white. Or, when he climbs up the fire escape to get Julia Roberts- That's what I want- swept off my feet. Is that too much to ask for?

AARON. Well, it is a little weird . . .

JOE. I guess that's why I'm still single.

AARON. But, what about Cory?

JOE. I don't know. We never seem to be in the same place at the same time. It's like we're doing <u>Sleepless in Seattle</u> and I got stuck in Newark.

PHIL. *(Returning from the bathroom)* If there is such a thing as reincarnation, I'm coming back as a loofah.

AARON. Did you get the Off? You are useless.

PHIL. You won't need those CD's. I made birthday mixes.

AARON. We should just go and leave the little, bleached blonde-

PHIL. *(Cutting him off)* No way. You can never have too much eye candy. And, it's natural.

> *There is a KNOCK on the door.*

AARON. Get that.

PHIL. *(Letting CORY in)* Hi Cory, we missed you last night.

CORY. Hi. Three waiters called in sick. It was a nightmare.

AARON. Hi Cory. I would think that as the owner, you could take a little time off.

CORY. Well, you know. *(After an awkward silence)* I just came up to get the cat.

JOE. I think he's still in the bathroom.

PHIL. *(Darting into the bathroom)* Oh, I'll get him!

AARON.   I'm going to go down and pull the car around, OK? *(Yelling to Phil)* I can see you.

PHIL. *(Off Stage)* I'm not touching anything - that's not mine.

AARON. Listen for me. I'll honk, OK? Bye Cory.

CORY. See you Saturday . . .

AARON. *(Stopping him)* Sunday. We don't get back 'till Sunday.

> *AARON takes the bags and exits.*

JOE. Thanks again for watching the cat.

CORY. Not a problem.

JOE. I'm sorry about earlier.

CORY. You got nothing to apologize for.

JOE. I left some DVD's for you on the counter. I couldn't remember where you left off.

CORY. Dark Victory.

PHIL and TRENT return from the bathroom. PHIL hands the cat carrier to CORY.

TRENT. *(To CORY)* Hi again.

CORY. Does he even own a shirt?

PHIL. God, I hope not.

CORY. Well, you guys need to hit the road.

CORY sneezes.

JOE. Bless you. Don't forget these.

CORY. *(Picking up the DVD's)*   Joe's got me working through the Bette Davis Collection.

CORY sneezes again.

JOE/PHIL/TRENT. *(In unison)* Bless you.

CORY. Thanks. Oh, and Joe, You have a real nice birthday OK?

JOE. Thanks.

CORY exits.

PHIL. Bye Cory. Where's Aaron?

JOE. Getting the car.

PHIL. Oh God, we gotta hurry. You know how he is about double parking - zero to freak in five seconds.

TRENT. I'm ready.

PHIL. I wouldn't have pegged Cory for a Bette Davis fan.

JOE. He didn't even know who she was 'till I gave him some movies.

PHIL. Come on. You have everything?

TRENT. I think Cory was checking me out.

JOE. He was not.

PHIL. I think he was checking me out, too.

TRENT. He was probably checking out that shirt.

PHIL. *(Exiting)* I'll have you know this is from International Male.

TRENT. *(Exiting)* Who's Bette Davis?

Blackout

Act One
Scene Two

JOE, TRENT, PHIL, and AARON are in their car. JOE and AARON are in the front seat. PHIL is in the back singing along to the CD.

TRENT. Could you at least change the station? I don't know how you can stand this shit.

PHIL. It's a CD. And, show some respect. She is our American Idol.

TRENT. My ass is on fire.

AARON. I'd think you would be used to that.

JOE. I told you this wouldn't be fun.

TRENT. Don't touch me.

AARON. *(Turning off the music)* Are you feeling better?

JOE. No.

PHIL. Nothing like a road trip. We haven't done this in a while - not since we drove to Detroit to see Cher's third final tour.

TRENT. I don't really care for her.

PHIL. Freak!

ONSTAR VOICE. Prepare to take a soft right in 200 yards.

AARON. Thank you, Vicky.

PHIL. Do you mind if I stretch out a little?

TRENT. Yes, I do.

AARON. I am going to separate you two.

ONSTAR VOICE. Go straight for the next 287 miles.

PHIL. *(Laughing)* That's not going to happen.

AARON. Thank you Vicky.

TRENT. Why does he keep calling her that?

AARON. Because that's her name. Vicky Lester.

JOE. A Star is Born. It's a movie.

TRENT. Never saw it.

AARON. Freak.

PHIL. Put the music back on.

AARON. No one can decide on what kind, so we'll just ride quietly.

PHIL. *(After a moment)* It's too quiet. Let's play again. Paul Walker in The Fast and The Furious. Come on.

JOE. Too young.

AARON. He was beautiful.

JOE. Richard Gere in An Officer and a Gentleman.

PHIL. He always says "Richard Gere."

AARON. Too 80's. Hugh Jackman in X-Men.

PHIL. Those sideburns are a turn off.

AARON. I think they're kinda sexy.

TRENT. I don't get it.

AARON. It's just a game Phil made up. You gotta name an actor you think is really hot and the movie he's in.

TRENT. How can you win?

JOE. You can't.

TRENT. Then, it's not a game.

PHIL. Yes, it is.

TRENT. I don't think you grasp the concept of a game. If you can't win, what's the point?

PHIL. The point is . . . the point is . . . OK, there is no point.

TRENT. See? It's not really a game. It's just stupid.

AARON. Will you quit bickering? Come on Trent, winning isn't everything. It's just a way to pass the time. It's fun.

TRENT. OK, but it's not a game.

JOE. It's your turn.

TRENT. I don't know. Ryan Reynolds in <u>Amityville Horror</u>.

PHIL. That ax is a turn off. Colin Farrell in <u>Alexander</u>.

JOE. That hair is a turn off. Paul Newman in <u>Cat on a Hot Tin Roof</u>.

AARON. The crutch is a turn off. Eric Bana in <u>Troy</u>.

TRENT. Brad Pitt is a turn off. Jake Gyllenhaal in –

PHIL/AARON/JOE. *(In unison)* <u>Brokeback Mountain.</u>

TRENT. Never saw it.

PHIL/AARON/JOE. *(In unison)* What?

TRENT. I was going to say <u>Donnie Darko</u>.

JOE. You are a freak.

PHIL. Let's see . . . Gerard Butler in <u>300</u>.

AARON. Anyone in <u>300</u>.

JOE. That is the gayest straight movie ever made. If you see another filling station, could we stop?

PHIL. God, this car smells like an old jock strap. And I don't mean that in a good way.

TRENT. Jeeze, it's creeping my way now. It's like a fucking gas chamber back here.

JOE. I'm sorry. It was the White Castle.

PHIL. Unlock the windows and let some air in.

TRENT. How fast are we going?

AARON. The speed limit. The last thing we need is a ticket.

TRENT. We're not going to get a ticket.

PHIL. Yeah, we're not even going fast enough to get a breeze. I swear, I can see bugs on the side of the road and they are passing us.

AARON. Shut up.

JOE. What kind of bugs?

TRENT. Speed it up. I'm starting to get light-headed back here.

AARON. I'm ignoring you.

JOE. *(Holding his stomach)* Maybe you could push it up a little.

AARON. *(Hitting the accelerator)* Oh, for God's sake.

Blackout

Act One
Scene Three

The deserted parking lot of a gas station. TRENT and AARON are waiting by the car. Throughout the scene, AARON tries to study a road map with his flashlight.

AARON. I still can't believe I got that ticket. Who the hell gets pulled over for going 58 miles an hour?

TRENT. At least that cop was cute.

AARON. What is taking them so long?

TRENT. Joe is still in the john and Phil is flirting with the cashier.

AARON.   That guy looks like he stepped out of Deliverance.

TRENT. *(After a silence)* How long have you and Phil been together?

AARON. Eight years. We've known each other about twelve. I sell pharmaceuticals. That's how we met. He's a nurse. He used to always let me sneak in to see the doctors. Enough with the questions. What's your story? Why are you really here?

TRENT. Joe invited me.

AARON. *(After a silence)*   And?

TRENT.   I'm kind of in between places right now and I didn't have any plans for the weekend. Besides, I like Joe. He talked to me last night. He really talked to me

AARON.   Why don't you have friends your own age?

TRENT. I don't know. I work a lot. George is pretty shy. When I'm Trent, it's easier.

AARON. How long have you been dancing?

TRENT.   A few months . . . My real job is at Starbucks. I'm saving up to go back to DePaul next year . . . to law school. I'm not as dumb as you think.

TRENT takes out a joint and starts to light it.

AARON. Is that pot? Did you bring pot?

TRENT.   Relax.   We're in the middle of nowhere at . . . what is the name of this place? The Filler-Up Stop. No one cares.

AARON.   In case you weren't aware, pot is illegal. We've already been pulled over once tonight. And, what if we get into an accident? We could go to jail.

TRENT.   If we get into an accident, we could get killed. Wouldn't you rather die stoned? You want a hit? It'll be our little secret. *(As TRENT lights the joint, AARON shoots him an evil look.)* I get the feeling you don't
like me.

AARON.   Listen . . . I don't know if Cory is still going to show up. But, if he does, you have to keep your distance from Joe.   We've been trying to get them together for months.

TRENT. You sure you don't want a little? It seems a shame to waste it.

AARON. Give me that.   The last thing we need is for Phil to find out you've got pot. He's hard enough to deal with when his brain isn't percolating.

> *AARON takes the joint from TRENT, who walks to the back of the car.*
>
> *AARON starts to pitch the joint, looks at it for a moment and then checks to see if TRENT is watching him. Sensing that the coast is clear, he takes a long drag. TRENT pretends not to notice.*

PHIL enters carrying a quilt, a soda and a bag of Twizzlers.

PHIL. What are you doing out here in the dark?

AARON. *(Startled)* Nothing. *(Pitching the joint)* I didn't have anything in common with Jethro in there.

PHIL. Look, he sold me this quilt. I think he made it. And, his name is Clem.

AARON. Clem. Sounds like something that gets caught in your throat.

PHIL. I wish. Any luck with Cory?

AARON. I left another message.

PHIL. Where's Trent?

TRENT. Back here. Taking a piss.

PHIL starts to try and sneak a peek.

AARON. Freeze. Where is my soda?

PHIL. Want a Twizzler?

AARON. I wanted a Dr. Pepper.

PHIL. I'm sorry. I forgot. I'll get you one. Do you have a dollar?

AARON. Why do you never have any money? Here. And, check on Joe.

PHIL. Last time I walked by, it sounded like he was giving birth in there.

PHIL exits.

AARON. This quilt was made in China. Look at the tag.

TRENT. Did you know I am from Tennessee?

AARON. How would I know that?

TRENT. I was just making conversation.

AARON.   Your family still live around here?

TRENT.   Yeah. But my folks and I aren't really what you would call "close" right now. My coming out didn't go too well. They closed my college account and I got kicked out of the dorm.

AARON.   You wanna try and see them? We could try and stop if it's on the way. Maybe you guys could try and patch things up. I can check with Vicky.

TRENT.   Wow, are you being nice to me?

AARON.   Just be careful with Joe, OK? I don't wanna see him get hurt again. I just wish Cory and him would finally hook up. He talks about him all the time. Cory did this. Cory said that. It's just that neither one of them will make a move. From what I can piece together, Cory's last boyfriend died in a car wreck and he hasn't dated since. It's obvious that he likes Joe. They are both just so fucked up. But, if all goes well this weekend -

> *PHIL enters.*

PHIL.   Here's your drink. *(Checking his watch)*   Man, it's late. We were supposed to be checked in by three.

AARON.   It's because we keep stopping! And, I think Vicky is confused.

PHIL.   Vicky is fucked up. It doesn't matter. They'll hold our rooms. I'll bet they are kissing our asses the entire weekend.

TRENT.   And, why is that?

PHIL.   Well, when I told them that Joe works for the Tribune - somehow - through the course of the conversation, I think they got the impression he's a travel reviewer.

AARON.   I wonder how that happened.

TRENT.   What does he do?

PHIL. He edits obituaries and sells classified ads. Anyway, the guy kept talking about how they love publicity and would really appreciate a good write up. That's how we got the discount price. Oh, and if it comes up, I am a doctor. Shh. Here he comes.

JOE. *(Entering)* That bathroom is disgusting. They have a spittoon in there.

PHIL. Let's hit it.

TRENT. How about letting me take the wheel for a while?

AARON. No . . . that's Ok.

PHIL. Yeah, maybe we can make up some lost time.

AARON. *(Finally)* OK. I'll read the map.

PHIL. Something stinks.

JOE. It wasn't me. I swear.

AARON. You're just not used to smelling fresh air.

PHIL. Hmm. It smells like pot.

ONSTAR VOICE. Prepare to turn right at the next intersection-

AARON. Oh, I think Vicky is working again.

ONSTAR VOICE. Or left.

BLackout

Act One
Scene Four

The four are still in the car. JOE is stretched out and asleep in the back seat.

AARON. You can tell a lot about a person from their eyes. They say they're the "Windows to the soul."

PHIL. Could this conversation be anymore boring?

AARON. Shh. Don't wake him.

PHIL. He hasn't made a sound for over an hour, from either end.

TRENT. We read an article in our Psych class about eye color and its' relationship to personality traits.

PHIL. Boring.

TRENT. Let me see if I can remember it.

PHIL. Boring.

TRENT. "Brown eyes symbolize sharpness; Blue Eyes, sweetness."

PHIL. Boring. Call me old fashioned, but I'm a dick man.

TRENT. No, you're a dick head.

JOE. *(Waking up)* What's so funny?

AARON. Welcome back. You've been asleep for almost two hours.

JOE. God, I feel so much better. Are we almost there?

TRENT. We have to be close.

JOE. It's so deserted.

TRENT. We haven't passed any other cars for miles.

PHIL. Hey, look up there . . . in the road. What is that?

AARON. Slow down. It's probably a deer.

JOE. If that's a deer, it's waving at us.

TRENT. It looks like a person.

PHIL. It is a person.

JOE. It's a hitchhiker.

PHIL. Oh, let's pick him up.

AARON. Absolutely not!

PHIL. He looks cute.

AARON. Trent, do not stop this car!

PHIL. Slow down then. Let's moon him.

JOE. What are you, twelve?

AARON. I think he's wearing a prison uniform. Lock the doors. Ignore him. Don't make eye contact.

PHIL. *(Waving as they pass)* We should have given him a ride. He looked gay.

AARON. Everyone looks gay to you.

ONSTAR VOICE. Go right on Juniper Junction for one quarter of a mile to your destination.

JOE. If this place is so great, you'd think they would have billboards or something.

AARON. The only signs I've seen are for the Tennessee Correctional Facility. Look, there's another one up there.

PHIL. That's it!

TRENT. What?

PHIL. Follow that arrow.

AARON. Into the prison?

PHIL. It's not a prison anymore. They converted it.

JOE. Into a spa?

PHIL. Yes, this is it!! This is Euphoria. We're here. Can you believe it? This is going to be great.

AARON. This can't be it.

ONSTAR VOICE. You have reached your destination.

AARON. But, there's a gate - an electric gate.

TRENT. Look at that wall. It's so high.

PHIL. Oh, it looks even better than it did in the pictures.

AARON. Is that barbed wire?

JOE. It looks so deserted. And, so gray. This can't be it.

PHIL. I tell you, it is. I recognize it from the web site.

AARON. I think I see someone coming.

PHIL. He's cute.

TRENT. I'll say.

> *As PATRICK approaches, the men get out of the car.*

PATRICK. Good evening gentleman. Welcome to Euphoria. We expected you hours ago.

AARON. We got a little lost.

PATRICK. Well, you made it. That's all the matters. We've now got you assigned to C-House.

PHIL. C-House. I like the sound of that.

PATRICK. We're almost done with the renovations, so you should find it acceptable. If you will just give me your car keys.

AARON. No. That's OK.

PATRICK. I insist. We have a staff to take care of everything. *(AARON hands him the keys)* If you gentleman will follow me, we'll get you processed.

PHIL. Processed? I like the sound of that, too. This is gonna be a blast.

PATRICK. My aunt and uncle run the spa. I'm Patrick Gunderson.

AARON. Hi, I'm Aaron Lang.

PATRICK. Nice to meet you, Mr. Lang. And, you are?

JOE. Oh, sorry. Hi, I'm Joe March.

PATRICK. It's an honor to meet you Mr. March. We were all alerted to your assignment.

TRENT. Hi, I'm George Willows.

PATRICK. Hello George. I'm sorry. I don't see your name here.

PHIL. It was a last minute addition. I hope it's not a problem.

PATRICK. There really are no problems here at Euphoria. But, you will have to bunk with one of your friends, at least for the first night.

PHIL. It's OK with me.

AARON. He's not staying in our room!

PHIL. Trent, I guess you're sleeping with Joe again.

PATRICK. I thought you were George.

TRENT. I am. We're not a couple.

PATRICK. Is this your Father?

JOE. No.

PATRICK. So, you must be Dr. Aherene . . .

PHIL. Guilty. But, you can just think of me as your Auntie Mame. *(PHIL takes PATRICK'S arm and starts to lead them all off stage.)* Oh Patrick, I'm going to open doors for you . . . . doors you never even knew existed. What times we're going to have - what vistas we are going to explore together . . .

BLackout

Act One
Scene Five

The common room of Euphoria. This was obviously a prison, but a rough and rather cheap attempt has been made to make it look like a resort. The sides of the room are lined with eight former cells, all labeled with room numbers. There are two hallways leading off stage. On the back wall, a large French door overlooks the grounds. The former guard station now serves as the check in area. The room also has a television, a couch, a few chairs and a small desk station.

MARIE'S VOICE booms over the public address system.

MARIE'S VOICE. Attention guests of Euphoria . . . This is Marie. If you want to participate in the Bondage for Lovers Workshop, you must sign the sheet posted in the commissary. The showers will be closing in forty minutes. Attention C-House, prepare for new arrivals.

PATRICK leads JOE, AARON, TRENT and PHIL into the common room.

PATRICK. If you'll just hang here, I'll go find my Uncle Donny and get your kits.

PATRICK exits down the hallway.

AARON. Well, the first thing they need to do is fire the decorator.

TRENT. I can't believe that woman frisked us.

PHIL. I think she was a he.

AARON. I want my cell phone back.

JOE. What chat room were you in when you heard about this place?

PHIL. I'm trying to remember.

JOE. I always said I wanted to visit Oz, but this isn't the one I meant.

> *GLEN casually strolls into the room. He is naked. A bag of pork rinds shield his nudity from the audience.*

GLEN. Want a pork?

PHIL. *(Taking a pork rind)* Thanks.

AARON. PHIL!

PHIL. I'm hungry.

GLEN. *(Seductively to JOE)* What about you? You look like you've got a healthy appetite. Dig in.

JOE. I'm fine.

GLEN. Well, I look forward to seeing a lot more of you.

> *GLEN exits into his room.*

JOE. OK, we should drive back to Memphis and get a hotel.

PHIL. But, we just got here.

JOE. I didn't like the way that guy was looking at me.

> *DONALD enters.*

DONALD.   Good evening gentleman.   Welcome to Euphoria. I'm Donald Gunderson. Sorry I wasn't able to greet you at the gate. But, it's been a crazy night, crazy. As you might have noticed, some of the wings are still under construction, so please pardon our dust. Now, let's get you processed. *(Handing them clipboards)* First, you must sign these release forms. In the unlikely event that something should happen, we can not be held responsible. Then, I will give you your cell - room assignments.

JOE.   You'd have to be an idiot to sign this without a lawyer.

PHIL. *(Handing in his signed form)* Here.

DONALD. Initial here please. Dr. Aherne, you are in cell #106.

JOE. Doctor?

PHIL. Shhh. Thanks.

JOE. Maybe we should leave . . .

AARON. We have to at least stay through tomorrow.

JOE. Why?

PHIL. Come on. This will be fun.

TRENT. *(Handing in his form)* Yeah, live a little.

DONALD. Thank you Mr. Willows.   We've got you in #107. It's nice. It has a window.

TRENT. Thanks.

PHIL. Come on Aaron. Sign your form.

AARON.   It is getting late. And, I don't want to drive anymore.

DONALD.   Initial Here. Mr. Lang, you are also assigned to room 106.

PHIL. Great, we're cell mates! You can be my bitch. Come on, Joe.

> *Just as JOE starts to sign the form, TINA opens her door, pops her head out and screams.*

TINA. Don't sign it!

TINA slams her door.

JOE. What the . . .

DONALD. Please ignore her. Initial Here. Oh, Mr. March, we have also placed you in room 107 . . .with your . . . friend. We originally had you in the East House. It's the one reserved for V.I.P.s. But, that group from CNN showed up again. Oh, here comes Patrick with your supplies.

> *PATRICK enters carrying a bag of toiletries and standard issue clothes and towels. He distributes them to the men.*

PATRICK. They're one size fits all.

JOE. Oh, that's OK. I brought my own stuff.

TRENT. I'll take one.

AARON. Where is our luggage?

DONALD. You won't be needing any of your possessions.

AARON. That's ridiculous. Where are my car keys?

DONALD. Per the contract, your car is not to be released until Sunday.

PHIL. Is this polyester?

DONALD. You signed the contract. And, you initialed it.

JOE. There was no way we could have read that. It was the size of a phone book.

DONALD. You came here to relax and you're going to relax.

JOE. But, this is kidnapping.

DONALD. No, this is C-House. If you follow the rules, we'll get along fine, and you will leave feeling better than you have in years. "A healthy mind equals a healthy body." My wife Marie and I try to live by that motto.

AARON. Donny and Marie?

PATRICK. Relax, he's harmless.

JOE. But, he's got a gun.

TRENT. This is the South. Everyone has a gun.

DONALD. Upon your release, if you are not happy, your room fees will be cheerfully refunded.

PHIL. That sounds fair.

PATRICK. And, no one has ever asked for a refund.

DONALD. In addition to our mineral, steam and mud baths, we have a sauna, a whirlpool, a complete gymnasium and workout facility and about twenty five specialty classes including, fishing, archery, arts and crafts and golf. We have a staff of 27, and 316 current inmates - guests.

PHIL. This all sounds great.

DONALD. And, some of you might enjoy our full line of adult oriented classes.

PATRICK. They're our most popular.

DONALD. "What happens here stays here." Per the contract, you must participate in a minimum of two classes or workshops per day. *(AGNES enters and stares coldly at the men.)* And, all of your meals will be supervised by Agnes, our resident nutritionist. When this was still a functioning penal institution, she was an inmate. She liked it here so much, when she made parole she decided to stay on. She is the trustee of C-House.

PATRICK. If you need anything, she is the woman to see.

DONALD. I must caution you, she is firm. They don't call her the Iron Maiden for nothing.

AGNES exits.

PATRICK. You've also arrived at a great time. Tomorrow we're holding our monthly dance, the Saturday Night Fever out on the lawn. Last month Marie was able to book two of The Four Seasons.

DONALD.   Tomorrow should be just as good.   Now, before you turn in, I want you to quickly meet your house mates. *(Yelling)* Prepare to stand your gate.

> *DONALD blows his whistle, making a series of different sounds.   With each sound, LORETTA, ALBERT, AIMEE, HEATHER and GLEN come out of their rooms and form a single file line.*
>
> *DONALD inspects the line, takes out his whistle and repeats one of the signals.*
>
> *TINA comes out of her room.*

TINA. Was that my signal? *(Taking her place in line)*   I can't get used to this.

PHIL.   This is just like The Sound of Music.

AARON.   Shut up.

DONALD.   Attention. We have a few late arrivals.   Why don't you quickly introduce yourselves and tell us how you came to be our guest?

ALBERT.   I'm Albert. My company sent me here in lieu of termination.

GLEN.   We've already met. I'm Glen Frugley.   I'm bi-curious. I found this place on The Bi-Lingams Website.

PHIL.   That's where I heard about this place!   Oops.

AARON.   We'll talk about that later.

PHIL.   I thought it was for people who wanted to learn English.

LORETTA.   Howdy, I'm Loretta. I'm in for arson.

AIMEE.   I'm Aimee Ruth. I couldn't afford an Olympia Cruise. And, this is Heather.

HEATHER.   Oh, I'm not with her. I like men. They just don't seem to like me. I'm here to lose weight. Ten more pounds to go.

DONALD. And, this is Mrs. Shouse. She's here on her honeymoon.

TINA. My husband, Troy escaped this afternoon. He'll be coming back for me. I just know it.

DONALD. Oh, Frau Hausmann picked him up a while ago. He was on the highway trying to catch a ride.

TINA. Oh, no.

AARON. I think we passed him.

DONALD. Gentleman, sound off. Doctor Aherene?

PHIL. Oh, call me Phil. I'm really glad to meet you all. I know we're all going to have a great time and probably become life-long friends.

AARON. Shut up.

DONALD. Dr. Aheren is one of Chicago's most respected brain surgeons. And, you are?

JOE. What is he talking about?

TRENT. I'm George. I'm here for Joe's birthday.

PHIL. Go, on. It's your turn.

AARON. This is ridiculous. I'm Aaron. I'm here because my boyfriend is a pervert and can't stay out of internet chat rooms.

PHIL. I'm the boyfriend.

DONALD. And, I am very happy to introduce you all to Mr. Joseph March from Chicago. He is the one I was telling you about. He works for the Chicago Tribune . . . the reporter.

The guests respond with tepid applause.

JOE. Why are they clapping?

PHIL. It's your birthday.

DONALD. And, why don't you tell us how you came to choose our humble establishment.

JOE. I'm here because I'm spineless and can never say "No."

GLEN. Hi Joe.

DONALD. You may all return to your rooms. *(The guests retreat into their rooms.)* We have discovered that incarceration can be a very freeing experience.

JOE. That doesn't make any sense!

AARON. Nothing about this place makes any sense.

PATRICK. Think of it as sort of an adult Disneyland.

JOE. But, I didn't want to go to Prison World.

DONALD. Patrick will provide you with a list of the classes and workshops along with a list of our rules and regulations. I trust you will read them over, but I just need to reiterate the major C-House rules. *(PATRICK hands each one of them a huge book.)* Number One - No switching rooms. Number Two - No Smoking or Drinking anywhere in the compound. If you respect your body, it will respect you. Number Three - Contact with the Outside World is strictly prohibited. Number Four - We cater to a large variety of people and fetishes. Always treat staff and guests with courtesy and respect. We do not judge and we do not photograph. And, Number Five - Clothing must be worn at all times in C-House common rooms and the cafeteria. Health code. But out there - on the grounds, behind those walls, clothing is forbidden.

JOE. What?

DONALD. This is a coed nudist resort.

AARON. You booked us into a nudist camp?

PHIL. I don't know. Maybe.

TRENT. What's the big deal?

JOE. I'm not taking my clothes off! Did you see the way Glen was looking at me?

DONALD. Except for special events, clothes are not permitted outdoors. This rule is strictly enforced by the staff, as well as Mimsey, Louise, Turk and Rudy.

PATRICK. They're the guard dogs. They have free run of the camp. Trust me. If they see clothes . . . It was on the release form that you signed.

DONALD. And initialed!

MARIE'S VOICE. Donald, report to the West Wing immediately. There is a 5150 in the macramé studio.

DONALD. Gentleman, I must leave you now. If you want a shower, you still have a little time. Mr. March, if you are in need of anything, please let us know. *(Exiting)* See you in the morning. Good night.

JOE. What is this place?

AARON. I have no idea.

JOE. Is it a prison? Is it a nudist colony?

PHIL. I know. I know. It's a penal colony!

> *PHIL and TRENT laugh.*

AARON. *(To Trent)* Don't encourage him.

JOE. I think we should go home.

AARON. Joe. . .

JOE. Really, I just want to go home.

PHIL. Why don't you try clicking your heels together?

AARON. Shut up.

PATRICK. My Aunt and Uncle mean well. They always wanted to run a health spa, and when the State closed this prison and he lost his assistant warden job, they were able to get the place cheap. They just can't quite decide what type of spa this should be. So, they try to appeal to a broad crowd, too broad. But, they are trying.

TRENT. I think it's kinda cool.

PATRICK. The Tribune isn't the only paper to send reviewers. The Advocate did a small article and overnight reservations doubled. And, we do get a lot of famous guests. I shouldn't tell you this, but Christianne Amanpour checked in again today.

JOE. You're OK with this?

AARON. I don't know. I love her. It's already so late. We're in the middle of nowhere. It's dark. I'm exhausted. They have the car . . the phones. . . Let's just stay tonight. We can try to sort this out tomorrow.

JOE. But, would you look in here? This room can't be any bigger than eight by eight. And, there is a toilet . . . in the middle of the room. And, only one bed.

TRENT. We're not a couple.

PATRICK. You told me, twice.

PHIL. We have bunk beds. I get to be on top.

PATRICK. He was serious about the showers. If you want one, you better go now. The water shuts off automatically.

AARON. Let's just shower and go to bed.

PATRICK. It's right down the hall to your right. You should have everything you need in your kits.

JOE. Fine. But, this is the last surprise getaway that I am ever going on.

PHIL. *(Looking in his kit)* Oh look, I got Tresemme'.

AARON. Come on.

JOE. I hate community showers.

PHIL. No one is going to look at you.

JOE. There better not be bugs.

AARON. Phil, come on. We need to stick together. *(Looking in his kit)* I got Paul Mitchell.

JOE. *(Looking in his kit)* I got Suave.

AARON, PHIL and JOE exit.

PATRICK sits down at the table to study.

PATRICK. Aren't you going to join your friends?

TRENT. They're really not my friends. Well they are but, we just met last night. Long story. What are you working on?

PATRICK. Just catching up on a little homework. I have to be back at school on Monday.

TRENT. What are you studying?

PATRICK. Law.

TRENT. Me too! Want some help?

PATRICK. No. You're on vacation. *(AGNES rushes in from one hallway and darts down the other towards the showers.)* Agnes, you know the rules. The men's shower is off limits.

TRENT. That woman looks deranged.

PATRICK. She's really pretty sweet.

TRENT. How long have you worked here?

PATRICK. I just help out here on weekends sometimes. Donny and Marie are a little more liberal than my folks.

TRENT. Oh. You got a girlfriend? Must be a lot of girls around here.

PATRICK. I guess. You can watch TV if you want. There's some DVD's in that cabinet. Those are my uncle's. I'm more into comedies.

TRENT. What's your favorite?

PATRICK. I love Ruthless People.

TRENT. I know that one. So, you're a Bette Midler Fan?

PATRICK. No. Danny DeVito.

TRENT. Oh. But you do like her music, right?

PATRICK. I'm more into The Rolling Stones. What?

TRENT. Nothing. So, what do you do for fun around here? You play sports?

PATRICK. Some. I like baseball.

TRENT. What team do you play on?

PATRICK. What?

TRENT. Never mind. But . . . you do work out, right?

PATRICK. Not really. I do like to swim. *(After a pause)* No more questions? You're done fishing?

TRENT. I'm sorry. I'll let you study.

PATRICK. Yes. No. And, yes.

TRENT. What's that?

PATRICK. The answers to the questions you're trying to ask. Yes, I'm gay. No, I'm not seeing anyone. And, yes I think you're pretty cute, too.

> *AGNES rushes back in carrying a stack of clothes and darts off down the other hallway.*

TRENT. That woman is crazy.

PATRICK. No, she a thief. She just stole their clothes. *(Yelling after her)* Agnes . . .

BLackout

Act One
Scene Six

The Common Room of the spa. PATRICK'S books are still on the table, but the room is now deserted.

TINA enters from the hallway and checks to make sure the room is empty. She darts down the hallway and immediately returns carrying a large coil of rope. She takes the rope into her room, comes back out and heads off again down the hallway.

PATRICK comes out of his room, returns to the table and resumes his studies.

After a moment, JOE, PHIL and AARON enter from the hallway. Their hair is wet and they are now dressed in their State issue casual attire.

PHIL. It shut off just as I was stepping out.

JOE. I've still got Suave in my hair.

AARON. How could someone take our clothes?

PATRICK. It's Agnes. Don't worry. I'll get them back.

JOE. Where's George?

PATRICK. I think I scared him off.

AARON. Well, we're going to turn in. We're exhausted.

PHIL. I'm not tired.

JOE. We're leaving first thing in the morning.

AARON. We'll see. Come on, Phil.

PHIL. You staying up?

JOE. For a bit.

PHIL. *(Looking to AARON for permission)* Please.

AARON. Fifteen minutes. *(To Joe)* Keep an eye on him.

> *AARON exits into his room and closes the door.*

PHIL. What do you wanna do?

JOE. I just want to sit down. I feel like I'm trapped in some sort of bizarre Lifetime movie. I keep expecting to see Judith Light.

PATRICK. Who?

TRENT. *(Entering)* What are you all doing out here?

JOE. I'm having a mid-life crisis.

TRENT. *(Holding up a joint)* Will this help?

PHIL. Yes!

PATRICK. How did you get that by Agnes?

TRENT. Want some?

PHIL. Yes!

JOE. Don't tell Aaron. I'm supposed to be baby-sitting.

TRENT. *(Opening the French doors)* We should go out here.

PATRICK. You can't. You're dressed. I can see Mimsey waiting there in the dark. If she's there, that means Turk is there, too.

> *TRENT takes a step out. The SOUND of DOG BARKING can be heard.*

TRENT. Shit!

> *TRENT quickly steps back in. The BARKING stops.*

PATRICK. I told you.

PHIL. I don't believe it. *(PHIL takes one step out. The dogs BARK. He quickly steps back inside. The BARKING instantly stops.)* I believe it.

PATRICK. They used to be with the K-9 squad.

JOE. Give me that. Maybe it will help me fall asleep.

PATRICK. You better keep this hidden from Agnes. She runs a little black market business on the side.

PHIL. My turn. My turn.

> *LORETTA comes out of her room.*

LORETTA. I smell smoke. Give me a drag of that.

TRENT. But, it's not a cigarette.

LORETTA. *(Taking it)* I don't care what it is. God, that's good. Thanks.

JOE. You're welcome. I'm sorry, I forgot your name.

LORETTA. I'm Loretta Holt. Loretta June Holt.

JOE. Hi, I'm Joe and this is George.

PHIL. And, I'm Phil.

LORETTA. Nice to meet you again. Oh, Happy Birthday, honey.

JOE. Thanks. And, I think you know Patrick.

LORETTA. Sure do. *(They take turns passing the joint around.)* This your first time here?

JOE. Yes . . . and last. How about you?

LORETTA. Lord no. I've been yo-yoin' in and out a here for the last couple a weeks. See, my husband Chet has been all over my ass to quit smokin'. He kept tellin' me that if I didn't quit he was gonna divorce me. So, I did try to quit, but it's hard. I even drove over to Dyersburg to have Garleen Potts try and hypnotize me. They say she has the "Gift." It didn't take. But now, for some strange reason, I can't stand creamed corn. Anyway, right after the fire, Chet threw me in the pick-up and dropped me off here.

JOE. Fire?

LORETTA. Yeah, I burned down my mother in law's place. Oh, it was an accident. If I had done it on purpose, that old bat would be toast.

PATRICK. Wow, you could put Agnes out of business. Her stuff is crap compared to this.

TRENT. What are you doing?

PHIL. Pot makes me horny.

JOE. Shh. Stand still. You're gonna wake up that Mrs. Danvers creature.

TRENT. Who?

JOE. That scary Nurse Ratched woman.

PATRICK. Who?

JOE. Doesn't anyone watch movies anymore? Never mind. Sorry Loretta, go on.

LORETTA. Pass that my way. *(After a long drag and silence)* I forgot what we was talkin' about.

TRENT. You were talking about a fire.

LORETTA. Oh, yeah. To make a long story short, we were over at Bootsie's place, that's Chet's mom. Her real name's Betsy but everyone calls her Bootsie on account of when she was a baby, she kept swallowin' her socks. Anyway, Chet had passed out on the sofa again and Bootsie was drivin' me crazy. So, I disappeared into the john to sneak a smoke. I needed to calm my nerves. I thought I threw the butt out the window, but I must've missed. The shower curtain went, the towels went, the bathroom went, and then whole the trailer went.

JOE. That's terrible.

LORETTA. And, Bootsie would not let it go. She said she was gonna press charges . . . said it was all my fault that she was trailer-less. The only way Chet could calm her down was to tell her he was gonna get me some professional help. He made me cancel all my appointments and checked me in here. Tell you the truth, it's better than bein' at home. Bootsie is staying with us till her new trailer comes. She ordered it special from Galesburg. If all goes well, I will be paroled tomorrow.

JOE. Smoking is a nasty habit.

LORETTA. I know. Pass it back.

JOE. Shh. Will you stop that?

TRENT. He keeps touching my ass.

PHIL. I do not!

PATRICK. Sorry.

LORETTA. Hey Patrick, can I ask you a question about your Aunt and Uncle? Which one is a little bit country and which one is a little bit rock and roll?

JOE and LORETTA burst out laughing.

TRENT. I don't get it.

LORETTA. You're probably too young.

JOE. Or, we're too old.

45

LORETTA. Speak for yourself. This is almost gone. So, you all fags or what? *(PATRICK, TRENT and JOE burst out laughing.)* I knew it. I can spot you fellows a mile away. I'm a hairdresser by trade. Went to beauty college with a bunch of homos. Maybe you know some of 'em. Joe Thebes?

JOE. Doesn't ring a bell.

LORETTA. Chester Martin?

TRENT. Sorry.

LORETTA. Claude Ott? Surely you know him.

JOE. I'm afraid not.

TRENT. Me neither.

LORETTA. Earl Wilton?

JOE. Loretta, all gay guys do not know each other.

LORETTA. Jack Thompson? You gotta know him. Six three, weighs about one twenty, red hair and buck teeth.

TRENT. I know him. He works at the Hair Cuttery in Lakeview.

LORETTA. See! It is a small world after all. Oh, no more. I know my limit. I'm gettin' kinda woozy. Last time I got really stoned was at Chet's brothers wedding. I stood up and objected. My sister-in-law still hates me. For some reason, almost everyone in Chet's family hates me. *(Yawning)* I think I better turn in.

JOE. We should think about hitting it, too.

PATRICK. But, it's early.

LORETTA. They wake you up here at the crack of dawn. Thanks again. 'Night. Don't let the bed bugs bite.

> *LORETTA returns to her room and shuts the door.*

JOE. Bugs?

TRENT. It's just an expression.

PHIL. I'm so thirsty. I can't feel my tongue.

JOE. Stop it.

PHIL. It feels so heavy. Is it moving?

PATRICK. There's a water fountain down that hallway and to your right.

JOE. If you're not back in three minutes, I'm waking Aaron.

PHIL exits off down the hallway.

PATRICK. Hey, I've got an idea. Let's go down to the lake and catch a swim. It's a perfect night out.

TRENT. Are you serious?

PATRICK. *(Starting to undress)* Come on. It'll be fun.

TRENT. What are you doing?

PATRICK. The dogs . . . They will attack.

JOE. I think I'll take a rain check. But, you boys go. Have fun.

PATRICK. Haven't you ever gone skinny dipping before? Don't be shy.

TRENT. *(Embarrassed)* I think I'll pass.

PATRICK. *(Taking off his shirt)* Oh, come on. It's not that late.

JOE. You should go.

TRENT. I'm kinda tired, too.

> *PHIL returns from the hallway with a cup of water.*

PHIL. Hey, What are you doing? I leave for a second and you decide to strip?

JOE. They're going swimming.

TRENT. I'm not swimming.

PATRICK. Come on.

PHIL. Go back and start again.

JOE. Go to bed.

PHIL. But, I want to see his . . .

JOE. Go to bed.

PHIL. Does something like this happen every time I leave a room?

JOE. I'm gonna get Aaron . . .

PHIL. *(Making a dramatic exit)* <u>Dead Man Walking</u>.

> *PHIL exits into his room and closes the door.*

PATRICK. I'm not gonna beg. Last chance.

TRENT. Maybe some other time.

PATRICK. Suit yourself.

> *Just as PATRICK is about to drop his shorts,*
> *AGNES enters from the hall carrying a piece of*
> *drywall. The drywall is just large enough to*
> *obscure PATRICK'S nudity from the audience.*

AGNES. This construction is going to be the death of me. What's that smell? Do you smell something burning?

JOE, TRENT & PATRICK. *(In unison)* No.

> *PATRICK exits out the French doors.*

> *AGNES exits down the hall.*

JOE. How come you didn't want to go swimming? I thought you guys were hitting it off. He's pretty cute, don't you think? *(Pause)* You didn't want to take your clothes off in front of him. You were embarrassed. That's it, isn't it?

TRENT. Shut up.

JOE. You like him. You do, you really like him.

TRENT. Seriously, shut up.

JOE. Make me.

> *JOE exits into his room and closes the door.*

> *TRENT knocks on GLEN'S door.*

GLEN. *(Opening his door)* Yes?

TRENT. I just thought you should know that my friend Joe thinks you're hot.

GLEN. The birthday boy? Really?

TRENT. He's in 107 and he's alone.

> *GLEN enters JOE'S room.*

JOE. *(Off Stage)* Get Out *(GLEN is ejected from the room.)* And stay out!! *(To TRENT)* Very funny.

TRENT. I warned you.

MARIE'S VOICE. Attention guests, lights out in fifteen minutes.

> *JOE and TRENT exit into their room and shut the door.*

> *GLEN knocks on ALBERT'S door.*

ALBERT. *(Opening his door)* I'm straight.

> *ALBERT slams his door.*

> *GLEN enters PHIL and AARON'S room and shuts the door.*

> *TINA enters from the hallway. She checks to make sure the room is deserted, goes back into the hallway and returns carrying a small ladder. She takes the ladder into her room and closes the door.*

AARON. *(Yelling from off stage)* He's not staying in our room!

> *GLEN is ejected from the room, returns to his own room and shuts the door.*

> *From off stage, JOE SCREAMS and immediately comes out of his room carrying a pillow and blanket. TRENT follows him into the common room.*

TRENT. You gotta be kidding.

JOE. I'm not! I'm not sleeping in there.

TRENT. *(Holding up a tiny bug)* But, it's just a moth and it's dead.

JOE. I don't care. It may have living relatives. I'm crashing out here.

TRENT. Fine. That just leaves more room for me.

> *TRENT exits into his room.*

> *JOE sits down on the sofa.*

> *GLEN opens his door.*

GLEN. *(Entering)* Did you change your mind?

JOE. NO.

GLEN. OK. *(Knocking on TINA'S door)* Tina? It's me, Glen.

TINA. *(Opening her door)* I told you to stay away from me. I'm married.

> *TINA slams her door.*

> *GLEN knocks on AIMEE and HEATHER'S door.*

AIMEE. *(Opening her door)* I'm gay.

AIMEE slams her door.

GLEN.   This bisexual thing is hard.   Twice as many rejections.

> *GLEN goes back into his room and closes his door.*

> *HEATHER opens her door.*

HEATHER. I'm available.

JOE. You just missed him.

> *HEATHER closes her door.*

> *AGNES enters with a rolling cart full of contraband and knocks on LORETTA'S door.*

LORETTA. *(Off Stage) (Yelling)* Go away Glen.

AGNES. Housekeeping. It's me, Agnes. Shipments in.

LORETTA. *(Opening the door)* What have you got?

AGNES. *(Holding up a pack of cigarettes)* A hundred bucks and I'll even throw in a lighter.

LORETTA. Got any Doritos? I got the munchies.

AGNES. No.

> *LORETTA slams her door shut.*

> *AGNES knocks on HEATHER and AIMEE'S door.*

AIMEE. *(Off Stage)* Glen, I am going to kick your ass.

AGNES. It's me. At night, all cats are gray.

AIMEE. *(Opening her door)* Oh, thank God. You got Heather's Pringles?

> *AIMEE hands AGNES some money, grabs a bottle of liquor and a can of Pringles and slams her door.*

AGNES. You need anything? How about a couple of dolls to help you sleep?

JOE. No. I think I am all set.

AGNES. If you change your mind, it's cash only.

AGNES scurries off down the hall.

JOE turns on the television. The SOUND of a VERY BAD PORNO MOVIE can be heard.

ALBERT opens his door and steps out to investigate the noise.

ALBERT. Would you mind turning that down? I have to be up early for interpretive dance.

JOE. Oh, Sorry.

JOE hits the mute button.

ALBERT returns to his room.

HEATHER enters from her room, with her and a large sketch pad.

HEATHER. Hi. I'm Heather, in case you forgot.

JOE. Hi. Joe. Joe March.

HEATHER. Joe March? Just like <u>Little Women</u>?

JOE. It's my mother's favorite book.

HEATHER. Mine too!! Can you believe it? Joe, Meg . . . and Marmee! I just love your whole family. I'll bet this is some kind of sign, don't you? We were destined to meet. Want a Pringle?

JOE. Thanks. I am a little hungry. God, this is good.

HEATHER. What are you watching? Oh, this is <u>Homo On The Range</u>. I saw this yesterday. Do you mind if I ask you a favor? Could you look at my drawing and give me your opinion? I have to turn it in for art class tomorrow.

JOE. Sure. Let me see.

HEATHER. It's not very good, is it?

JOE. I'm no expert, but I don't think any woman would be shaped like that. Look how large this breast is compared to this one. See how low it hangs? You probably could have used a model.

HEATHER. I had one. It's Aimee. What classes have you signed up for?

JOE. I'm not taking any.

HEATHER. You have to take at least two. It's in the contract. I do recommend crochet. And, the cooking classes are OK.

JOE. We're leaving in the morning.

HEATHER. Oh. Well, if you change your mind, Dr. Drew is going to give a lecture on the female orgasm. I think he was on Oprah once. How come you're sleeping out here all alone? You have a fight with your boyfriend?

JOE. He's not my boyfriend.

HEATHER. So, you're available?

JOE. I'm gay.

HEATHER. Oh, OK. I thought so. What about your friends?

JOE. Sorry.

HEATHER. It figures. All the good guys are either married or gay.

JOE. They must be married.

HEATHER. I thought that this might be a good place to meet men. Wrong! So far, the only offer I have received has been from my roommate Aimee. I just don't get lesbians. I don't think we have any in St. Louis. I mean, what can one woman see in another woman?

JOE. I don't even know what men see in women.

HEATHER. I know I am a little overweight. But, I am trying to control what I eat. *(Eating a Pringle)* I figured that if I lost a little weight, someone might notice me. I'm just big-boned.

JOE. I think you're very attractive.

HEATHER. That's 'cause you're gay. Gay men don't mind chubby girls. They just don't like chubby guys. Why is that?

JOE. I don't know.

HEATIIER. I have a good personality. That's what my Mom always tells me. When someone mentions your personality, you know you're in trouble. You want a soda? I think they keep some behind the desk.

JOE. Oh, that would be great.

HEATHER. My friends keep telling me that I've got to put myself out there, that there's plenty of fish in the sea. Well, I brought my fishing pole. I just hope I've got the right bait. I don't think this is soda. *(Reading)* Skinny Gazelle. Oh, it's an energy drink. It's not very cold.

JOE. I don't care. I'm just so thirsty.

HEATHER. So, do you have a boyfriend?

JOE. I was dumped. Jeff came home from school and announced that he had rented out our spare bedroom to one of his twenty five year old grad students. I guess I don't have to tell you what they were studying.

HEATHER. Men are pigs.

JOE. Jerks.

HEATHER. Bastards.

JOE. Assholes.

HEATHER. But, I still want one.

JOE. Me, too. I do have someone that I am interested in. But, he's not here.

HEATHER. I have my eye on someone, too. And, he's in there. *(Pointing to ALBERT'S room)* He's so cute in that nerdy insurance salesman kind of way. *(Toasting with the Pringles)* To us. I'm sorry. I'm getting crumbs all over your bed. I sleep out here sometimes, too. We just have a single in there and Aimee likes to cuddle.

MARIE'S VOICE. Attention guests of Euphoria, there is a heat advisory for tomorrow. If you are participating in any water sports, retain plenty of fluids. Prepare for lights out.

HEATHER. I better get in there. Aimee's got some of Agnes's home made hootch. She gets a little forward when she drinks. I gotta go layer up. It was nice talking to you. Oh, if you mention me in your article, please make me ten pounds lighter.

> *HEATHER goes back into her room and closes the door.*
>
> *JOE turns off the television.*
>
> *After a moment, TINA creeps out of her room, carrying the coil of rope, an ax and a small ladder. She places them on the floor near the French doors, returns to her room and comes out again with her gym shoes.*

JOE. Hello.

TINA. *(Startled)* Oh, I didn't know anyone was out here.

JOE. It's just me.

TINA. Well, I'm busting out of this joint. You wanna come?

JOE. Oh, I don't know.

TINA. I've been collecting this gear all day. Those contractors just leave stuff lying around. *(Putting on her shoes)* Can you believe this place? It's nothing like that ad in <u>Southern Bride</u>. Romantic honeymoon retreat my ass. Have you ever heard of a resort that won't let the bride and groom share a room? And, the things they do in those classes. Nasty. With this ladder and rope, we should be able to shimmy over the wall.

JOE. What about the dogs?

TINA. I was on the track team in high school. And, I did have a Skinny Gazelle with my dinner. You with me?

JOE. No. We're gonna leave in the morning.

TINA. If I don't make it, when you write your article, could you please say that I died a married woman?

> *TINA picks up the ladder, rope and ax and steps outside.*

JOE. *(Looking out the window)* Oh, no. Here they come. Look behind you

TINA. *(Off Stage)* Good Mimsey. Pretty Mimsey. What a nice doggy. *(The DOGS begin to BARK.)* Oh, shit.

JOE. Don't move.

> *The DOGS are SILENT.*

TINA. *(Off Stage)* What do I do now?

JOE. On the count of three, make a run back here. One, Two, Three. I said "Three."

TINA. *(Off Stage)* I can't. You've got to come out here and get me.

JOE. What?

TINA. *(Off Stage)* Please.

> *JOE cautiously steps out the French doors.*

The DOGS begin to BARK furiously.

AGNES rushes in to investigate the commotion.

AGNES. What the hell? For God sakes, stand still. *(The DOGS are SILENT.)* What are you doing out there with your clothes on?

JOE. *(Off Stage)* I have a problem saying "No."

AGNES. Is that Tina with you?

TINA. *(Off Stage)* Hi.

AGNES. Well, the Midnight Express is not taking off on my watch.

LORETTA, ALBERT, GLEN, AIMEE and HEATHER come out of their rooms.

ALBERT. What's all the commotion?

AGNES. Everyone get away from the window.

AIMEE. Yeah, what's all the noise? We were trying to spoon.

HEATHER. Hi Albert.

TRENT enters.

TRENT. What's going on?

LORETTA. Tina and Joe are makin' a break for it.

AGNES. Just stand there and let her gum you! Everyone, get back to your cells. There is nothing to see here.

The DOGS begin to BARK.

GLEN. I'll get them. Help me undress.

EVERYONE. No!

AGNES. Freeze! Now, everyone just stand still and be quiet.

57

EVERYONE is silent.

DOGS stop BARKING.

Suddenly, MOANING can be heard coming from PHIL and AARON'S room.

AARON. *(Off Stage)* *(Singing)* "Ah, sweet mystery of life at last I've found you . . ."
   The DOGS begin to BARK again.

AGNES. Oh, shit! We need back up.

AIMEE. *(Yelling)* Tina, Bring me the ax.

AGNES. *(On her walkie talkie)* Code 399.5. Repeat Code 399.5.

   As the BARKING, SCREAMING and MOANING continue, AGNES hits the switch on the wall. The ALARM SOUNDS.

MARIE'S VOICE. Attention guests of Euphoria, lights out.

BLackout

END OF AcT ONE

Act Two
Scene One

The common room of the spa. It is now early morning. JOE is lying on the couch.

The door to AIMEE'S room opens and she peeks out. Slowly, AGNES comes out of the room and disappears down the hallway. AIMEE closes the door.

MARIE'S VOICE.   Attention guests of Euphoria . . . Today's breakfast; scrambled eggs with a sun dried tomato and baked bean medley with sea bass and a side of tartar - is compliments of our visiting guest chef, Tom Colicchio. Special Note - due to an unidentified fungus, today's Kama Sutra Mud Wrestling Course has been cancelled.

> *The door to ALBERT'S room slowly opens and HEATHER and ALBERT come out. ALBERT is dressed in makeshift dance attire, complete with leg warmers.*

HEATHER. The food goes quick here.   You coming?

JOE.   No thanks.

> *HEATHER heads off down the hallway to breakfast.*
>
> *ALBERT does a few dance moves and exits down the other hallway.*
>
> *JOE crosses to the French doors and opens the curtains. GLEN is outside doing aerobics. He is naked.*

GLEN. *(Outside)* Good morning!

JOE quickly closes the curtains.

JOE. *(Knocking on Phil and Aaron's door)* Aaron? Phil? Are you guys awake? Guys, get up.

AARON. *(Opening the door)* Shh. I don't wanna wake Phil.

JOE. What's with you two, anyway? The entire prison heard you last night.

AARON. I don't know what's gotten into him. We started talking about all the sick, disgusting things that have probably happened in that cell and he got really turned on. I think it has something to do with all the concrete.

JOE. Too much information. Look, we gotta see about getting the car back.

AARON. Joe, I am going to ask you to do something. Before you say "No," please just listen. I want to stay.

JOE. What?

AARON. I know this place isn't exactly what we thought it would be. . but we . . . but I want to stay. Something changed when we got here. Phil's been-- Well, last night was the best sex that I have ever had.

JOE. I told you, way too much information.

AARON. It's only one more night. What do you say? You know I don't ask for favors very often. But, things between Phil and I have started to get a little . . . what is the word? Comfortable. But, this place has done something to him. On Monday, he will have to go back to that clinic. Don't you think he deserves to cut loose a little? Please. Do it for us.

JOE. So, I'm supposed to be the bad sport again? Joe is boring. Joe can never be spontaneous. Well, I'm sorry. This is not my idea of a great birthday. What am I supposed to do all day?

AARON. Let's all sign up for a class. Come on. It'll be fun. I swear. I will make this up to you. Just say "You'll stay."

PHIL. *(Entering from his room)* Good morning.

AARON. Hi.

JOE. What are you smirking about?

PHIL. Now, I finally know what Lionel Ritchie meant by Three Times a Lady. God, it's stuffy in here.

JOE. I wouldn't do that.

> *PHIL opens the curtains. GLEN is still doing his stretches*

GLEN. *(Outside the French doors)* Good morning.

PHIL. Wow, you are limber.

AARON. Do you have to do that right here?

> *AARON quickly closes the curtains.*

PHIL. Well, I'm gonna get something to eat. You coming?

JOE. No.

AARON. I haven't had anything to eat since those Twizzlers. You want us to bring you back something?

JOE. No.

AARON. We can talk about this after breakfast.

> *PHIL and AARON exit.*

> *AIMEE comes out of her room dressed in her robe.*

AIMEE. Morning. I'm going to try and run a few laps before my cosmetology class. Today is my final.

> *AIMEE starts to remove her robe.*

JOE. What are you doing?

AIMEE. I'm going outside . . . The dogs. . .

JOE. Oh, no. Please don't . . .

AIMEE. You got something against a woman's body?

> *Just as AIMEE is about to drop her robe, AGNES enters from the hallway carrying an oddly shaped piece of drywall.*
>
> *The drywall blocks AIMEE'S nudity from the audience.*

AGNES. Looking good.

AIMEE. Thanks. What are you staring at?

JOE. I was wrong. Heather's drawing was accurate.

> *AIMEE exits out the French doors.*

AGNES. Can you believe those workers would just leave this in my kitchen? *(Knocking on LORETTA'S door)* Hey, smoking beauty, you better get your gear together for inspection. Nobody gets gated out till the room passes my white glove. I'm gonna miss that dame.

> *AGNES exits and JOE returns to the couch and switches on the TV.*
>
> *LORETTA enters.*

LORETTA. What are you watching? Oh, <u>Homo On The Range</u>. You and Tina sure made quite a ruckus last night.

JOE. I'm so embarrassed.

LORETTA. Oh, don't be. How is my hair? I'm getting' sprung today and I need to look good for the outside world.

JOE. Take me with you.

LORETTA. You mind if I say something personal? You'd have a lot more fun if you'd just relax. Aside from the lack of cigarettes, I've had a pretty good time here. I've even lost a little weight. And, there's a lot of stuff to do. I learned a lot of new things - some of them I didn't really need to know. Don't sign up for beginning scat. It's not a music class. As my friend Juanita would say, this is one of those places where you just need to "Gump it."

JOE. I don't understand prison lingo.

LORETTA. You know, like Forrest Gump. Juanita's always saying "Go with the flow. Be a feather. Waft." She's got the right attitude about life. I admire her. It's gotta be hard to be a shampoo girl with only one arm. Now, let's see. There must be something that you would like to do. You like sports? They got volleyball and tennis.

JOE. I'm not going outside.

LORETTA. I'm a little shy too. Not that I got anything to be ashamed of. You probably haven't noticed, but I've got great boobs. And you could crack an egg on my ass. Hey, I'll bet if they offered a class in that, someone would sign up. It takes all kinds. You know, there's a guy down the hall that just likes to look at your feet. That's it . . . just look at them. Maybe before I leave I'll give him a quick peek. You like crafts? There's a beginning origami course and a class in Bedazzling.

JOE. I'm not very artistic.

LORETTA. Well, here's a class in organ grinding, but I wouldn't risk it. You gotta read between the lines with these classes here. Poor Albert signed up for wood working and he couldn't walk for two days. And, don't sign up for a facial. Something weird goes on in that room.

JOE. I think I will just lay here . . . all day long.

LORETTA. No offense, but you're kinda dull.

JOE. When did this happen to me? When did I get to be so old?

LORETTA. Honey, you aren't old. But, you keep thinkin' that way and you will be. I'm convinced, if you don't know how to have fun, it ages you. Your skin knows. It gets bored and starts to shrivel up.

JOE. Then, I must look about ninety.

LORETTA. No, you don't.

JOE. Last week, I went to the mall to buy some new pants for this weekend. I must have looked at fifteen different kinds until I found the one that I thought looked the best on me and was the most comfortable. It wasn't until I was taking them off in the dressing room that I discovered that they were Sansabelts. You know, the pants with the elastic waistband and no belt loops? I have started to like old man pants! I almost cried right there in the stall.

LORETTA. There is nothing wrong with comfortable pants. Elastic is God's way of saying "Go ahead, have another piece of pie."

JOE. And, you don't even want to hear about the hair that has started growing on my back.

LORETTA. No, you're right, I do not. Once we were in bed and Chet found a renegade hair growing out of my nipple. Did I let that ruin our night? Hell no! I plucked that sucker out quicker than you could say Naomi Judd and we went on about our business. You can't out run father time. If you could, I would be out of work. Now, let's quit talkin' about body hair and get you cheered up. There has to be something here you like to do. Think. What interests you?

JOE. Well, I like to go to the theatre and I like to watch movies.

LORETTA. I think we're on to something. There's a film discussion meeting today. They're screening <u>Teacher's Pet</u>.

JOE. I love <u>Teacher's Pet</u>. Wait, do you think it's the same one, the Doris Day one?

LORETTA. I'm sure it is. They use her song as kind of the spa anthem.

JOE. The thing is . . . the movie theatre is out there.

64

LORETTA. Think about what I said. Well, I need to run. I'm squeezing in a jewelry making class before Chet gets here. I'm going to learn to make a pearl necklace.

LORETTA exits.

TRENT and PATRICK come out of PATRICK'S room.

JOE. I don't think that no-switching-rooms rule is working.

TRENT. I was helping Patrick study, so I just crashed on the bottom bunk.

JOE. Well, let me bring you up to speed . . . Aaron and Phil don't want to leave.

TRENT. Oh, good. We're gonna grab some breakfast. I'm starving.

PATRICK. Why don't you come with us?

JOE. No.

TRENT. You need to loosen up. You're way too uptight.

JOE. I am not uptight!

TRENT and PATRICK exit off down the hallway.

JOE switches on the TV and stares blankly at the screen.

MARIE'S VOICE. Attention guests, if you were scheduled to attend the lecture on the female orgasm, Fire in the Hole, Dr. Drew has cancelled. However, he was kind enough to fax us his original speech, and Dr. Hiro Takahashi from the Memphis Community College will give the presentation.

The curtains at the French door ruffle and GLEN enters. He is carrying his exercise mat, which shields his nudity from the audience.

GLEN. *(Looking at the TV)* I'll bet if you held my legs up, I could do that.

JOE. *(Quickly changing the channel)* Will you put something on? I'm gonna report you to Agnes.

GLEN. Chill out, man. You got something against the human body?

JOE. That human body, yes.

GLEN. Well, I'm not the one sitting here watching porn at six in the morning.

JOE. I wasn't watching . . . Please go.

GLEN. You seem a little lonely. I just thought you might need a friend.

JOE. Look, I don't mean to be rude, but this is the last place on earth I would expect to meet any friends.

MARIE'S VOICE. Jennifer Aniston, report to the ceramics studio. Jennifer Aniston to the ceramics studio.

Blackout

Act Two
Scene Two

The common room of Euphoria. JOE, TRENT, and AARON are seated and casually crocheting.

AARON. You have to admit, that was an excellent lunch. Agnes certainly knows her way around a kitchen.

JOE. The crushed Cheetos were an interesting touch.

AARON. Maybe she'll give us the recipe.

> *PHIL enters from the hallway. His state-issued shirt has now been "Bedazzled."*

PHIL. You were right. That woman is definitely not Susan Lucci.

AARON. He keeps thinking he's seeing celebrities. He thought our waiter was Neil Patrick Harris.

PHIL. *(Taking his place on the sofa)* I'm still not convinced. Where were we? Oh, It's was your turn.

TRENT. I don't know Taylor Lautner in <u>New Moon</u>.

JOE. Too young. Jon Hamm in <u>Mad Men</u>.

TRENT. That's not a movie.

AARON. It doesn't matter.

JOE. OK. Jon Hamm in <u>Bridesmaids</u>.

PHIL. Hamm. Can you think of a worse last name for an actor?

TRENT. This game really sucks.

JOE. Let's just talk about something else.

PHIL. You're pulling that too tight.

TRENT. I've got it.

AARON. *(After a silence)* Well . . . What should we talk about?

JOE. *(After another silence)* Why don't we each discuss the last books we've read?

They are all SILENT.

PHIL. Do magazines count?

AARON. No. *(After an awkward silence.)* I can't remember the last book I read.

TRENT. Mine was <u>The Legal Environment of Business: Text and Cases</u> by Frank B. Cross. Wanna discuss that?

JOE/PHIL/AARON. *(In unison)* No.

JOE. I think the last book I read was <u>Harry Potter</u>. Hey, that reminds me of an article I was reading about in <u>TIME</u>.

PHIL. He said magazines didn't count.

AARON. Shut up.

JOE. It was about how scientists are working on a formula for invisibility. You know, like how Harry has that cloak? They say that in principle, it is theoretically possible to make one. They just haven't been able to put all the pieces together yet. That got me thinking.

AARON. About what?

JOE. Well . . . obviously these scientists are straight. Ask any gay man and he can tell you that invisibility is not only possible, it exists and occurs daily.

TRENT. I have no idea what you are talking about.

PHIL. Does anyone else think Harry Potter sounds like the name of a porn film? <u>The Hairy Potter Goes . . .</u>

AARON. Shut up. Go on Joe.

JOE. I figure it starts at around age 28. It's gradual at first, but each year you fade a little more. By the time you are 40 you are virtually invisible. Of course, there are some exceptions - like if you are still really thin. That buys you a little more time. But, if you start gaining weight, forget it. Fat actually accelerates the invisibility process.

AARON. I think you're exaggerating.

JOE. I'm not. When I walk into a bar, I'm like something out of H.G. Wells.

TRENT. That Daniel Radcliffe is kinda hot.

PHIL. The way he holds his wand . . . I'd do him.

AARON. You'd do a shoe. But, I must admit, those pictures from Equus were smokin'.

PHIL. I think it's pronounced Equus.

JOE. Can we stop talking about Harry Potter?

PHIL. Well, you brought him up.

JOE. The point I was trying to make is that I would rather spend the night at home with my DVD player than sitting in a bar trying to get someone to notice me.

TRENT. You're never gonna meet anyone that way.

PHIL. Don't forget to chain three when you turn that.

TRENT. When you told me I was going to make a pot holder, this isn't what I thought it would be.

AARON. That's going to be a pretty scarf.

JOE. Good, 'cause you're getting it for Christmas.

AARON. Does this look wrong to you?

PHIL. That depends on what it's supposed to be.

AARON. I was going for a dish towel.

PHIL. Then, it's wrong. *(PHIL helps AARON with his work.)* Pull out this bottom row.

AARON. See, Joe? Isn't this fun? All of us together on your birthday-

PHIL. OK, is everybody ready? One the count of three, turn your project. One, Two, Three . . .

The men flip their work and continue crocheting.

JOE. What exactly is that?

TRENT. It looks like a sling-shot.

PHIL. It's a thong.

JOE. What kind of freak would wear that?

AARON. That better not be for me.

PHIL. I'm sure I can find someone who will appreciate it. What time is it?

TRENT. Almost one.

PHIL. Don't forget, I signed us up for softball.

JOE. I'm not going outside.

PHIL. But, we took crochet class with you.

JOE. Forget it.

TRENT. Count me out, too. I'm meeting Patrick.

PHIL. Where is spa-boy anyway?

AARON. Yeah, what's up with you two?

TRENT. I don't know. I think he likes me.

AARON. Do you like him? *(Trent smiles)* Then, tell him. You want me to say something?

TRENT. Don't you dare.

PHIL. Give him that pot holder. If he accepts it without laughing, you're home free.

AARON. Well, I think it's nice that you've found a friend. See Joe? See what happens when you put yourself out there?

JOE. I am not going outside. I can't believe you're not embarrassed.

PHIL. I'm not ashamed of what the good-lord gave me.

JOE. He wasn't that good to you.

PHIL. It's not what you've got, but how you use it.

AARON.   Amen, sister. Actually, it's very freeing. And if you wear sunglasses, you can check out the guys and they can't tell.

MARIE'S VOICE.   Mr. Hiro Takahashi please report to the visitor's entrance.

PATRICK enters.

PATRICK. Hello.

TRENT. Oh, Hi. I'm almost ready. I just want to finish this row.

PATRICK. No rush. He's going to help me study.

JOE. Why don't you look over your Uncle's contract and find a way out of out here?

PHIL. OK. I can finish this later. I gotta get some sunscreen before softball. Hey Patrick, you do know that Trent has the hots for you, don't you?

TRENT. Shut up.

PHIL exits into his room.

AIMEE enters. She is wearing an ornately styled wig and has a very bad make-up job.

AIMEE. Hi guys. What do you think? I got a B+.

JOE. You look . . .

AARON. *(Cutting him off)* Very nice. Did you get contacts?

AIMEE.   I only need my glasses for really close up.

TRENT.   You need to work on not squinting.

AIMEE.   It's a wig. Can you tell? I was getting tired of my mullet. I was going for a softer look. Can't wait for the girls at work to see. You might not believe this, but there are a lot of butch gals at the Jiffy Lube. Agnes said I showed the biggest improvement in the entire class - Even more than Herbert Michelle.

PATRICK. He's the transvestite that teaches rumba. She's really good.

AIMEE.   I really like Agnes. We talked the entire night last night. And, her perfume is fantastic. It lingers.

AIMEE exits into her room.

JOE.   I haven't seen that many bows since the Eukanuba Dog Show.

TRENT. At least she's making an attempt.

JOE. What's that supposed to mean?

AARON. She's just trying to . . .

JOE. What? Fit in? If one more person tells me that I am uptight or that I need to put myself out there, I am going to cram this crochet hook down their throat.

AARON. I'm sorry . . . .

JOE. I've tried. I've put myself out there. I've gone so far out there that I've come back in!

PHIL enters.

PHIL. Did you change your mind?

JOE. Get out.

PHIL.   God, sometimes, I wonder why we hang with you. You have no sense of adventure.

JOE. I'm serious. Get out now.

PHIL. *(Hanging his robe on the hook)* Come on, Aaron. No wonder he had to pay for a date.

PHIL exits out the French doors.

JOE. What does that mean?

AARON. Nothing. Ignore him.

JOE. *(To TRENT)* Are you a . . . . ?

TRENT. No, I'm not.

PATRICK. What are you talking about?

TRENT. And, I returned the money.

PATRICK. What money?

TRENT. Come on. I'll explain it all. *(To JOE)* Here.
Maybe this will help calm you down.

> *TRENT places a joint and a lighter on the table and
> then exits down the hallway with PATRICK.*

AARON. Joe . . .

JOE. And, you can kiss that scarf goodbye.

AARON. I'm sorry, Joe. We were trying to cheer you up.
Lately, you've just been so . . .

JOE. Desperate?

AARON. Sad. Since your break up, you haven't been the
same person. We miss the old Joe.

JOE. The idea that you think I have to pay someone . . .

AARON. We don't think that. We keep hoping that you
and Cory will connect-

JOE. Well, so do I. But, if things are going to happen
between Cory and me, they will. The last thing I need is
you two butting in and playing some sort of matchmaker.

AARON. Well . . . About Cory. . .

JOE. I should have figured it out. Look at Trent. I could
never get that lucky.

AARON. Your life isn't a movie, Joe. I know you. You're still waiting for Richard Gere to come in here and sweep you off your feet.

JOE. I don't think he's coming.

AARON. Don't say that.

JOE. It's true. I'm twelve years old all over again. This is like the time you gave Billy Goldberg fifty cents not to pick me last in dodge ball. I got hurt that time too, remember? Sometimes, it's better to just sit the game out.

AARON. It isn't.

> *PHIL appears at the door.*

PHIL. Aaron, come on. Let him stay here and mope. He loves it.

AARON. He doesn't mean that.

PHIL. Yes, I do. You just love to wallow in it. You can't stand the fact that someone else may be having fun. When, you don't even try.

AARON. Phil . . . *(PHIL disappears out the door.)* Just ignore him.

JOE. Maybe he's right.

AARON. Phil's never right.

JOE. Go on. Go play your game. I'll deal with Philip later.

AARON. Are you sure?

JOE. Go.

> *AARON removes his robe, hangs it on the hook and exits out the French doors.*

> *JOE stares out the window. Forgetting, he takes a step out the door. Instantly, the dogs begin to bark. He steps back inside and notices the joint on the table. He makes sure the coast is clear, lights it and sneaks a smoke.*

ALBERT enters from the hallway.

ALBERT. That was a grueling final. That bean casserole I had for lunch didn't make it any easier. Agnes said I showed the most improvement - even better than Michelle Herbert. Would you like to see part of my dance? I call it The Re-Birth of a Claims Adjuster.

JOE. Maybe a little later. When this kicks in.

ALBERT. It starts with me all curled up in a fetal position, kinda like this. And, I'm laying in a pool of red light. Are you getting a visual? Now, picture if you will an enormous vagina. . .

JOE. Really, I'd rather not.

ALBERT. I think it was pretty good. Heather gave me a standing ovation. You better not let Agnes catch you smoking in here.

JOE. *(Looking out the window)* These people look ridiculous. Look at them, frolicking around the yard . . . Naked.

ALBERT. You probably look ridiculous to them. Did you think of that? It's a beautiful day and you're in here hiding behind the curtains and getting stoned. What are you afraid of Joe?

JOE. Well. . . I don't know.

ALBERT. I think you're afraid you might actually have some fun. What is that song you guys are always singing about, Don't Let the Parade Pass You In The Rain?

JOE. But, how can you go along with all this?

ALBERT. I was sent here by my company as kind of a punishment. Might as well make the best of it.

JOE. What happened?

ALBERT. I insulted an Eskimo. He called about some insurance quotes. While I was checking rates, I started cracking jokes with my co-worker. Stupid stuff. We wondered if igloos needed fire insurance. Or, if he would pay in blubber. I thought he was on hold. He wasn't. Did you know there is actually an Eskimo anti-defamation society? E.A.D.S. They wrote a letter threatening to sue, so I got sent here for sensitivity training. No one seems to have a sense of humor anymore. Have you noticed that?

JOE. Apparently, I'm the wrong person to ask about humor. You want a hit of this?

ALBERT. No. It's kinda early. I need to grab a book. Heather asked me to be her partner in something called Latex - Friend or Foe? I really like her.

ALBERT exits down the hallway.

MARIE'S VOICE. Attention guests, please be on the lookout for Mr. Hiro Takahashi. He was last seen at the entrance to C-House. If you see him, please direct him to the visitor's entrance. He is not dangerous. He is here to give a lecture.

PATRICK enters from the hallway.

PATRICK. I need to grab my practice exam. You shouldn't be smoking in here. *(PATRICK exits into his room and returns a moment later with his papers.)* Are you OK? You wanna talk?

JOE. No. George is waiting. Go have fun.

PATRICK. You wanna hang out with us this afternoon?

JOE. Great, now you're feeling sorry for me.

PATRICK. No, I'm not. But, your friends are really worried about you.

JOE. I'm fine.

PATRICK. If you change your mind, we'll be in the library.

JOE. Thanks. You go. Waft.

PATRICK. Excuse me?

JOE. Just some advice Loretta gave me. She said that I should be a feather.

PATRICK. Well, Good luck with that.

> *PATRICK exits.*

> *HEATHER enters from the other hallway carrying a cupcake with a birthday candle.*

HEATHER. Here. Anges whipped this up for you. Happy Birthday.

JOE. Thanks. I'm not really very hungry.

HEATHER. But, you gotta make a wish and blow out your candle. Come on. *(JOE blows out the candle.)* What did you wish for?

JOE. I wished that my friend Cory would . . .

HEATHER. Wait, don't tell me. It's bad luck.

JOE. My luck couldn't get any worse.

HEATHER. That's how I felt. But today, I have a whole new outlook. I think Albert really likes me.

JOE. He does. He told me.

HEATHER. Really? You just wait. It'll happen for you, too. You just gotta have faith. Are you gonna finish that?

JOE. Help yourself.

HEATHER. *(Taking the cupcake)* Trust me. Sometime, when you least expect it, that door will fly open and in will walk Mr. Right.

> *Just as HEATHER goes into her room and shuts the door, the French doors fly open and GLEN enters. He is naked and wearing a swimmer's mask, snorkel and life jacket. A pair of flippers shields his nudity from the audience.*

GLEN. That Agnes is one hell of a skier.

GLEN exits into his room.

JOE begins to LAUGH. It is a strange laugh, almost as if he is crying.

JOE. I think I'm having a nervous breakdown. Maybe it's the pot.

Suddenly, the lights go out. A single, bright spotlight illuminates JOE, as he sits on the couch. Throughout the following, the other actors enter, but remain in the shadows. We are hearing what JOE is thinking. This is JOE'S pot induced hallucination. The dialogue begins slowly and quietly. As the scene progresses, the volume and speed increases to a frantic pace. Dialogue gets faster, as the actors begin to overlap each other.

TRENT. He's kind of shy.

PHIL. He won't even change clothes at the gym.

AARON. Happy Birthday.

LORETTA. You'd have a lot more fun if you'd just relax.

HEATHER. Happy Birthday.

ALBERT. What are you afraid of, Joe?

TINA. Happy Birthday.

LORETTA. Life is too short.

PHIL. Let him stay here and mope.

AARON. We miss the old Joe.

DONALD. Happy Birthday.

LORETTA. Honey, you aren't old.

PHIL. Sometimes, I wonder why we hang with you.

TRENT. You need to loosen up.

GLEN. Happy Birthday.

LORETTA. But you will be.

PATRICK. Think of it as sort of an adult Disneyland.

AARON. It's very freeing.

TINA. The things they do in those classes.

ALBERT. You're afraid that you might actually have some fun.

LORETTA. You can't out run Father Time.

PHIL. You have no sense of adventure.

TINA. Nasty.

DONALD. What happens here stays here.

TRENT. Happy Birthday.

DONALD. This is a coed nudist resort.

GLEN. You got something against the human body?

PATRICK. Come on. What are you waiting for?

LORETTA. Your skin knows.

ALBERT. What is normal, anyway?

PHIL. I'm not ashamed of what the good-lord gave me.

LORETTA. Let's quit talkin' about body hair.

AIMEE. You got something against a woman's body?

AARON. See what happens when you put yourself out there?

PATRICK. Haven't you ever gone skinny dipping before?

LORETTA. Go with the flow.

PATRICK. Happy Birthday

PHIL. No one is going to look at you.

AIMEE. What are you staring at?

LORETTA. Be a feather.

TRENT. You're way too uptight.

LORETTA. Waft.

PHIL. They're all gonna laugh at you.

ALL. Happy Birthday.

DONALD. You get your strength from the red earth of Tara.

ALL. Tara! Tara! Tara!

JOE. *(Yelling)* ENOUGH! I get the message. *(The spotlight goes out and the normal stage lights return. JOE is once again alone on the sofa.)* Well, that was weird. Maybe they're right. *(JOE turns and stares at the French doors.)* Maybe they're all right.

> *JOE gets up, crosses to the French doors and looks outside. Summoning up his courage, he starts to undress. As he is about to drop his shorts, GLEN pops his head out of his room.*

GLEN. Joe, you going outside? Wait up. Let me get undressed and I'll come with you.

JOE. Oh, Shit!

> *JOE rushes out the door.*

> *GLEN returns to his room.*

MARIE'S VOICE. Mr. Takahashi please report to the women's studies wing. Your class is about to begin.

> *TRENT, PATRICK and CORY enter from the other hallway. CORY is carrying a box of chocolates, a bouquet of flowers, a bottle of wine and a small birthday balloon.*

PATRICK. He was just here.

TRENT. He's been here all day.

CORY. I'm supposed to find Aaron and Phil first. Joe doesn't know I'm coming. It's a surprise.

PATRICK. Then, you better wait here. My Aunt and Uncle have this policy about unregistered guests.

TRENT. We'll go try and find Aaron and Phil.

PATRICK. If you get into a bind, or hear someone coming, Loretta's room is vacant.

CORY. This is ridiculous. I'm not going to hide.

TRENT. You don't want to ruin the surprise, do you?

> *PATRICK and TRENT exit down the hallway.*

AGNES. *(Off Stage)* Mr. Takahashi? Paging Mr. Hiro Takahashi.

> *CORY panics and lays flat on the sofa to hide.*

> *AGNES walks thru the common room and off down the other hallway.*

DONALD. *(Off Stage)* I know I had a bucket of nails.

> *CORY sees the bucket of nails, panics and runs into AIMEE'S room to hide.*

AIMEE. *(Off Stage)* I'm a lesbian! Get out. *(The door opens and CORY is pushed out.)* But, I'll take that!

> *AIMEE grabs the wine bottle and slams her door.*

DONALD. *(Off Stage)* Maybe I left them in the hallway.

> *CORY panics and rushes into TINA'S room to hide.*

TINA. *(Off Stage)* I'm a married woman. *(The door opens and CORY is pushed out.)* I will take those flowers though.

> *TINA grabs the flowers and slams her door.*

> *HEATHER opens her door and sees CORY.*

HEATHER. Oh, sorry. I'm already taken. If things don't work out with Albert, I'll let you know. *(Taking the chocolates)* Thanks. You are pretty cute.

HEATHER exits off down the hallway to class.

DONALD. *(Off Stage)* Oh, I left them on the coffee table.

CORY. Shit!

CORY panics again and rushes into GLEN'S room to hide.

DONALD enters to retrieve the nails.

DONALD. I swear I would lose my head if it weren't attached.

DONALD exits down the hallway with the nails.

CORY immediately comes out of GLEN'S room. In addition to the balloon, he is now holding a large rubber sex toy.

GLEN. *(Looking out of his room)* I'm gonna need that back.

As GLEN closes his door, AGNES enters.

AGNES. Who are you?

CORY. I'm . . .

AGNES. Unregistered guests are not allowed in here.

CORY. *(Starting to panic)* But, . . . I'm . . . I'm . . .

AGNES. Oh, my goodness. You're Mr. Takahashi. You're here to give the lecture on the female orgasm.

CORY. No, I'm . . .

AGNES. We've been looking for you for hours. I thought you would be Japanese. *(Bowing to him)* Welcome. Welcome. You do speak English, don't you?

CORY. Yes, but I'm . . .

AGNES. Well, we've got to hurry. Here's a copy of your speech. I'm glad to see you brought visual aids.

> *AGNES grabs CORY by the arm and rushes him off down the hallway.*

BLackout

Act Two
Scene Three

AARON, PHIL, TRENT and PATRICK are in the common room. AARON is nervously pacing.

PHIL. You have got to calm down.

TRENT. The one I feel sorry for is Glen.

PHIL. How does one get hurt at a Doris Day movie?

TRENT. Well, I know Joe finally decided to go outside. He sat through Teacher's Pet and then participated in the discussion afterward.

AARON. I can't believe it.

TRENT. After the meeting, another film started, 9 1/2 Weeks. Now, I guess there is some sort of erotic refrigerator scene. And, apparently, it was audience participation.

PATRICK. They do that sometimes.

TRENT. A lot of people brought food. I guess Joe freaked out, jumped up and tried to leave.

PATRICK. The usher said that he slipped on some strawberries or honey or baked beans. She wasn't sure which, because the floor was covered in condiments.

AARON. He is never going to forgive us.

TRENT. He fell into a crowd of people on the floor. Finally, I guess Glen, who happened to be there, realized that Joe was actually injured. Somehow, he managed to pick Joe up and carry him out of the theatre.

PATRICK. Now, the rest of this I got from a woman who was playing tether ball. She said at first when she saw Glen running across the lawn with Joe in his arms, she thought it was kind of romantic, a kind of lover's game. Then, she noticed Joe screaming.

TRENT. Then, Glen tried to take a short cut through the croquet tournament. He didn't notice the game and tripped on one of the gates. Joe went flying

PATRICK. That's how he hurt his back and leg.

AARON. This is a nightmare.

PATRICK. At least he landed on the grass. Glen wasn't so lucky. He tried to catch himself, fell backwards onto one of the croquet poles and was semi-violated.

PHIL. Ouch.

TRENT. Amazingly enough, he seems to be doing OK.

PATRICK. They think that the honey acted as some sort of lubricant.

TRENT. Glen's just roaming the hallways trying to walk it off.

AARON. We have to try and get Joe home.

PATRICK. Well, I guess I could get you guys out of here, but he really should take it easy.

AARON. But, what about Cory? Where is he?

PATRICK. I told him to wait here, or hide in Loretta's room.

AARON. This sucks. This really sucks.

TRENT. Calm down.

AARON. Don't tell me to calm down. Cory is lost and Joe is hurt. This is all our fault.

PATRICK. If it will make you feel better, we'll go back down to the infirmary and check on him.

TRENT. How could you get us out of here?

PATRICK. I drafted the contract. I know the loophole.

TRENT. Why didn't you tell me?

PATRICK. I wanted you to stay.

PATRICK and TRENT exit down the hallway.

PHIL. You gonna let this one little thing ruin the rest of our weekend?

AARON. This is not a little thing.

PHIL. You're cute when you're upset. Sexy.

AARON. I am not! *(GLEN enters from the hallway.)* Oh my God, Glen. . . how are you feeling?

GLEN. I'm just trying to get over the shock of it all.

AARON. You want to sit down?

GLEN. I don't think I can.

PHIL. *(Trying not to laugh)* I'm so sorry.

GLEN. I just wasn't expecting that pole. I don't know how you gay guys do it.

GLEN wobbles off down the other hallway.

AARON. It's not funny. How would you like a wooden pole rammed up your ass? Don't answer that.

MARIE'S VOICE. Attention guests . . . The Saturday Night Fever and wiener roast will begin in thirty minutes. The dogs will be locked up as this is a clothing optional event.

AARON. Did you hear that?

PHIL. Everyone heard it. It was on the loudspeaker.

AARON. Not that, listen. It sounds like moaning. I think it's coming from Tina's room. *(Knocking on TINA'S Door)* Tina? Is that you? Are you OK?

TINA. *(Opening her door)* What? Oh, Hi.

AARON. Is everything alright?

TINA. Everything is great. Troy got to come back today. We went to Mr. Takahashi's lecture. Did you know there are over fifty positions? He gave us an illustrated handout. We'll try and keep it down.

TINA closes her door.

PHIL. There's something about this place. Have you noticed it? It seems to bring people together. Remember last night? Hubba Hubba. You were amazing. Now, Tina and Troy. And, Trent and Patrick.

HEATHER and ALBERT enter.

ALBERT. Hi guys. You going to the party?

PHIL. I hope so.

HEATHER. We are. Albert invited me.

ALBERT. She's an amazing girl.

HEATHER. Woman. *(Exiting into her room)* I'll just be a second.

ALBERT. Sorry to hear about what happened to your friend. Now, I feel kind of bad for telling him to get out there and enjoy himself. But, when I left him, he seemed OK - Just a little stoned.

ALBERT exits into his room.

AARON. That explains it. Trent got Joe stoned. That's why he went outside.

PHIL. Now, it's Albert and Heather hooking up. I tell you, it's this place. If we could only find Cory. . .

AARON. Where could he be?

PHIL. Calm down. You are going to hyperventilate.

AARON. He wouldn't just up and leave, would he? God, when will I ever learn? I think I am going to faint.

PHIL. You're not going to faint.

AARON. I'm serious. I'm feeling light headed. I'm going to faint. Get ready to catch me.

PHIL. Put your head between your legs. Breathe. Deep breaths. . . *(AARON bends down and takes a few deep breaths.) (PHIL is standing behind him and pushing his head down.) (GLEN enters from the hallway.)* Breathe in. Hold it. Now, blow. Blow. Are you blowing?

AARON. I'm trying. Nothing's coming out.

GLEN. *(Taking in the situation)* You gotta be really limber to do that. Trust me. I've tried.

> GLEN exits down the hallway.

AARON. Joe is going to kill me when he finds out we've lost Cory. Now, I think I'm having a heart attack.

PHIL. And, the role of the drama queen is being played by Aaron Lange.

AARON. I'm serious.

PHIL. You're not having a heart attack.

AARON. Don't tell me I'm not having a heart attack. If I say I'm having an attack, I'm having an attack! Feel my chest. I don't think my heart is beating.

PHIL. *(Feeling his chest)* I don't feel anything.

AARON. What? Can you hear it? Listen. *(Lifting his shirt)* It's stopped, hasn't it? It's actually stopped.

> Just as PHIL puts his ear to AARON'S chest, ALBERT comes out of his room.

ALBERT. Oh, sorry. *(Knocking on HEATHER'S door)* We'll be right out of here and you guys can continue whatever it is you are doing.

AARON. We're not doing anything!

HEATHER. *(Opening her door)* I'm ready.

ALBERT. You smell wonderful.

HEATHER. Thanks. It's White Diamonds. Agnes said it always brings her luck.

PHIL. *(Looking out the French Doors)* It looks like it's going to be a nice turnout. I hope there's dancing.

ALBERT. *(Doing a small dance move)* So do I.

AARON. How can you even think of dancing?

PHIL. *(Singing)* "God, I'm a dancer. A dancer dances-"

AARON. Stop that.

HEATHER. We better grab a seat. Come on. *(To Phil)* Albert doesn't think I'm fat. Come on Albert.

> *HEATHER and ALBERT exit out the French doors.*

AARON. I don't think you're taking this situation seriously. Joe could have been really hurt.

PHIL. But, he wasn't. Besides, you worry enough for the both of us.

> *AGNES and TRENT enter escorting JOE.*

AGNES. Let's get him on the couch.

AARON. Oh my God. . . . Joe.

TRENT. He's fine.

AGNES. Doc gave him a little something . . . a relaxant. He's just a little blazed.

AARON. Blazed?

PHIL. What's up with his hair?

AGNES. I don't think I got all the food out. I tried to give him a sponge bath, but he fought me every step of the way.

AARON. Joe, I am so sorry. Talk to me.

JOE. Baked bean medley.

AGNES. He's may be a little loopy for a while.

JOE. Sun dried tomato.

PHIL. He is out of it. Joe, how many fingers am I holding up? How Many? Joe, look at me.

AGNES. You don't have to yell at him.

JOE. Phil is an ass.

PHIL. He called me an ass.

AGNES. I think he said he can't feel his ass.

>   *JOE picks up the remote and turns on the television.*

PHIL. He's back to normal.

AARON. Joe, why don't we turn that off? You can watch TV later.

PHIL. That looks like <u>Homo on the Range</u>. *(Catching himself)* *(To Aaron)* OK, I rented it when you were out of town.

TRENT. I'm going to try and find Patrick. He went to look for Cory.

AGNES. Who?

AARON. No one. *(Turning off the TV)* Let's turn this off.

AGNES. His eyes are awfully red.

PHIL. It's probably the pot.

AGNES. What?

AARON. He's kidding. We don't have any pot.

AGNES. Do you need some?

AARON. No.

AGNES. Well, I've got to go help Michelle Herbert with the hors d'oeuvres. *(Knocking on TINA'S door.)* Hey, you two lovebirds, remember to stay hydrated.

>   *AGNES exits.*

AARON. I'm not sure he's breathing.

PHIL. He's breathing.

AIMEE enters.

AIMEE. You guys ready for the party?

AARON. No.

AIMEE. Oh, I don't like his hair like that. Do you want me to try and fix it? I don't mind. Is this a baked bean?

AARON. Just let him rest. This is all our fault.

PHIL. Don't start in again. *(To AIMEE)* I wish they would have sedated him.

AIMEE. *(Excited)* Oh, are you stressed out? Are you? I can help. Let me help!

AARON. What are you doing?

AIMEE. I've been learning the ancient Japanese art of Reiki. I'm taking a class at our Discovery Center. Now, don't be alarmed. I'm going to try to touch your Chi Spot.

AARON. No. Really, it's not necessary.

PHIL. Maybe she can help.

AARON. But, I'm fine.

AIMEE. *(Doing an elaborate ceremony with her hands)* Just relax. Take a deep cleansing breath. Feel the positive energy of your life force. Relax. Feel it. Let go of your stress. Relax. Feel it. Relax. Relax.

AARON. Thanks. I'm better now.

AIMEE. *(Yelling)* I said relax! Let yourself go. Relax. Let yourself go and . . .

PHIL. *(Cutting her off) (Singing)* "Relax. You've got yourself tied up in a knot. The night is cold but the music's hot . . ."

AARON. Shut up.

AIMEE. Feel the stress leaving your body. Oh, your life force energy is very low. This is not good. Tap into my energy. Tap. Tap. Tap.

PHIL. Are you tapping?

AIMEE. Prepare to receive the higher power. Feel the glowing radiance as it flows into you. It's flowing. Flowing. Do you feel the warmth?

AARON. Oh, yes, it's flowing. It's really warm, hot almost. You can take your hands off me now. Thanks. Wow, I feel a lot better. I feel great. Thanks a lot.

AIMEE. Don't mention it. You're the first person that I have really had a chance to try it on. Maybe I should try it on him. *(Laying her hands on JOE'S head)* Well, he's already pretty relaxed. I'll just give him a quick shot. I don't want to get drained. Relax. Relax. Tap. Tap. Flow. Flow. There, that ought to do it. Well, my work here is complete. Agnes asked me to be in charge of the bonfire and I gotta find some matches. Do you have any?

AARON. No.

AIMEE. Maybe Loretta left some in her cell. Namaste.

> *AIMEE exits into LORETTA'S room.*

AARON. Do you think we should try and lay him down? He looks uncomfortable. Help me.

> *PHIL helps AARON try to reposition JOE on the couch. They have a difficult time and he slides off onto the floor.*

PHIL. Careful. Lift with your legs. Spine fine, back crack.

AARON. Shut up.

PHIL. You shut up.

JOE. Sea bass. *(PHIL and AARON try desperately to reposition JOE back onto the sofa. As JOE'S body is contorted into a compromising position, he begins to mumble.)* Bass. Bass. Bass.

AIMEE comes out of LORETTA'S room and sees the three.

AIMEE. Disgusting!

AIMEE exits out the French doors.

AARON. This is not funny.   Would you help me?

PHIL and AARON try to reposition JOE on the sofa.

PHIL. He's just dead weight.

AARON. Lift his legs. Higher. Higher. .

GLEN enters from the hallway, and sees the men contorted into what appears to be another intense, acrobatic sexual position.

JOE. *(Moaning)* Tartar. Tartar. Tartar.

GLEN. I'll bet if you held my legs up, I could do that.

GLEN exits into his room.

As JOE slumps back down off the sofa, CORY, PATRICK and TRENT enter from the hallway.

TRENT. Look who we found sitting in a classroom.

AARON. Cory!

CORY. What are you doing? Joe are you OK?

PHIL. Hi Cory. He's asleep.

CORY.   Why is he on the floor?

AARON. We were trying to reposition him.

CORY. Let me help. Man, he is out.

They reposition JOE back up onto the sofa.

JOE. Scrambled eggs.

CORY. What?

PHIL. I think he's planning a menu.

CORY. He's going to be OK, right?

PHIL. He'll be fine.

CORY. I hate his hair like that.

AARON. Did they make you sign anything?

CORY. No.

AARON. Oh, thank God. Then, you can leave.

CORY. But, I just got here.

PATRICK. I gotta head back to the visitors entrance. I'm supposed to meet a Pip.

TRENT. What's a Pip?

PATRICK. You know, a Pip. Aunt Marie booked him to play the pavilion tonight. We couldn't afford Gladys. You coming?

TRENT. I'm right behind you.

PATRICK and TRENT exit down the hallway.

AARON. Cory, Joe still doesn't know that we. . . that I invited you.

PHIL. Yeah, I had nothing to do with it.

AARON. When he comes out of this, he's going to be pissed. But I take full responsibility.

CORY. Don't you think he would want me to be here?

PHIL. We didn't even know if you wanted to be here.

CORY. It's his birthday. Of course I want to be here.

PHIL. I'm sorry. I know this is none of our business. But, what the fuck is going on with you two? He likes you. You don't like him. You like him. He pretends he doesn't like you. It's really annoying. I mean, the Sam and Diane thing is so 1980's.

AARON. Phil . . .

CORY. No, it's OK.

PHIL. We are just so sick of this waiting for you guys to hook up. So, Lucy here decided to meddle. But, he only did it because he cares.

CORY. Would I have driven eight hours if I didn't really want to be here?

PHIL. It took us thirteen.

CORY. Look, I have had a rough couple of years. Since Brian died, everything seems to have fallen apart.

AARON. You don't have to explain. It's none of our business.

CORY. I never even thought about dating again until Joe moved in. But, when he first asked me out, it was just too soon. It didn't feel right. So, I just sort of threw myself into the restaurant.

PHIL. But, you do like him, right?

CORY. He's adorable.

AARON. Then, tell him.

CORY. Something always seems to get in the way.

PHIL. Well, I know he likes you.

CORY. He has to know that if I really needed a parking space, I could afford one. And, that damn cat of his. I hate that thing.

PHIL. How could you hate Ennis Del Mar?

CORY. I'm allergic. And, Joe has the worst taste in movies. I can't tell you how many of those he has made me sit through.

AGNES enters.

AGNES. *(Knocking on GLEN'S door)* Hey Glen, come out here a second. *(Seeing CORY)* Mr. Takahashi, what are you still doing here?

CORY. Oh . . . I'm . . . I'm . . .

AGNES. Well, you are certainly welcome to stay for the party. *(GLEN comes out of his room wearing PHIL'S crocheted thong.)* Herbert Michelle said he's saving you a seat and she can't wait to dance with you.

GLEN. Really? I thought I felt some sort of chemistry with him in rumba class.

AARON. Where did you get that?

GLEN. It was a gift.

AARON hits PHIL in the arm.

AGNES exits.

CORY. That woman scares me. She made me teach a class.

AARON. She made you what?

CORY. Teach a class on the female orgasm. Luckily, I only had two students. I had to keep saying "clitoris."

PHIL. It's pronounced "clitoris."

CORY. Are you sure? I think it's "clitoris."

PHIL. No, it's "clitoris." Just let it roll off your tongue.

AARON. Will you two shut up? You're making me nauseous.

GLEN. He looks so peaceful. I really like his hair like that.

CORY. Hey, leave him alone.

GLEN. *(To CORY)* Well, hello again.

JOE. Leave him alone.

97

AARON. You're alive!

GLEN. You were quite a handful this afternoon. How you feeling?

JOE. Never better. Hi Cory.

GLEN. I think I am good as new, too. I got the rest of the splinters out. I put a little of Agnes' makeup on to cover the bandages. Can you tell?

AARON. Quit looking at him.

PHIL. I'm sorry, but if there's a naked man standing in front of me, I don't care how hideous he is, I'm gonna look. Oh, I didn't mean that you were hideous; actually you have a nice-

AARON. Shut up.

GLEN. *(To CORY)* Hi, I don't think we've officially met. I'm in plumbing fixtures. I supplied all the commodes and sinks in B House.

CORY. Hi.

AARON. OK. Seriously, you need to leave, or put something on.

GLEN. It's clothing optional. *(To CORY)* I believe that you still have something of mine.

CORY. What? Oh, I loaned it to Tina.

AGNES enters.

AGNES. Come on, Glen. You know how Michelle Herbert is about tardiness.

GLEN. If you ever need your plumbing looked at, call me.

AGNES. You should try and come outside. The party should be a humdinger. Kevin Spacey brought his ukulele.

CORY. Kevin Spacey is here?

PHIL. Can you settle something once and for all? Is he gay or straight?

AGNES. Yes, he is.

AGNES and GLEN exit out the French doors.

JOE. Don't you have something you want to say?

AARON. Joe, I am so, so sorry.

JOE. Not you. You.

CORY. Happy Birthday. I brought you some presents, but people kept taking them.

AARON. Please don't be mad. It's not his fault. I invited him here to surprise you.

CORY. Surprise.

JOE. I'm not mad. I heard the whole thing. That was the most fun I've had in weeks, listening to you guys fumble around.

PHIL. Did you call me "an ass" ?

JOE. Aaron, why don't you take Phil outside? I want to talk to Cory.

AARON. And, you're really not mad?

JOE. This is shaping up to be a pretty good birthday.

PHIL. It's clothing optional, what do you say?

AARON. I say we keep our clothes on - until later.

PHIL. Hubba Hubba. There is definitely something about this place.

AARON and PHIL exit out the French doors.

CORY. Look, I'm really sorry about all this. About your birthday-about us. You want to just try and start things over again?

TINA enters from her room.

TINA. Sorry to interrupt. We need some water. We're up to number ten and Troy is starting to dehydrate. Oh, Mr. Takahashi I can't thank you enough. Are you gay?

CORY. Yes.

TINA. All the knowledge. . . . ?   What a waste.

TINA exits down the hall.

JOE. You don't like my movies and you don't like my cat.

CORY. But, I do like you. What do you say? Would you like to go out with me?

TRENT and PATRICK enter.

TRENT. I heard you were awake. So, you guys cool, or what?

JOE. We're cool.

TRENT. I'm going to ride back with Patrick tomorrow, if that's OK.

JOE. I think that's great.

TRENT. You guys really should come out here.

PATRICK. Yeah, the Pip is about to start.

TRENT. I caught Agnes and Aimee sneaking a kiss.

PATRICK. I think it's sweet.

TRENT. I think you're sweet. Joe, I'll probably be staying in Patrick's room again tonight.

TRENT and PATRICK exit out the French doors.

JOE. Nothing happed between us.

CORY. I know. I could hear the vomiting.   *(A COMMOTION can be heard down the hall.)* This place is a zoo.

LORETTA and DONALD enter.

DONALD. We are very disappointed in you, Loretta. We expected more from a licensed beautician.

100

LORETTA. What can I say? Bootsie sniffed me out. She's got a nose like a bloodhound. Actually, she's got the face of a bloodhound, too.

DONALD. Your old room has not been re-assigned yet. Take it.

LORETTA. Who's your friend?

DONALD. Yes, who are you? You're not supposed to be in here. Are you with the band? Are you a Pip?

JOE. Does he look like a Pip? He's a friend of mine.

DONALD. Mr. March, non-registered guests are not permitted here, especially during Saturday Night Fever. You're going to have to register.

CORY. OK, I guess.

DONALD. I'll get your list of rules and regulations.

> *DONALD takes CORY to the registration desk.*

JOE. Loretta, I took your advice. I'm wafting.

LORETTA. I can see that. He's cute. I'm going to unpack. Oh, and Joe? Don't take the jewelry class.

> *LORETTA exits into her room.*

CORY. Wow, this is some registration form.

> *TINA returns from the hallway with a glass of water.*

TINA. Just sign it, Mr. Takahashi, sign it!

> *TINA exits into her room and slams the door.*

DONALD. Mr. Takahashi? I got the strangest call about a Mr. Takahashi. He's down the street at The Our Lady of Fatima Convent trying to give a lecture and it's not going well. *(CORY signs the contract.)* I hope you don't mind bunking with your friend. Is that OK, Mr. March?

JOE. Look here. He forgot something.

DONALD. You missed this part, the one about the escape clause.

JOE. Initial it.

CORY initials the form.

MARIE'S VOICE.   Attention guests of Euphoria, The Saturday Night Fever has begun. If you want a hotdog, bring your buns to the gazebo.

DONALD. Mr. March, you really should cover this for the paper.

JOE.   I am not a reporter.

DONALD exits out the French doors.

CORY. Well, what do we do now?   Want to watch TV?

JOE. I think I've had enough TV for a while.

GLEN enters from outside.   He is walking very slowly and holding a towel over his crotch.

GLEN. If you go out there by the fire, stand upwind.

GLEN exits off down the hallway.

JOE. I think that guy is accident prone.

CORY. What do you say?   You want to go to a wiener roast?

JOE attempts to stand.

JOE. I guess I am a still a little groggy.

CORY. I could carry you.

JOE. Oh, right.

CORY. I could do it.

CORY attempts to lift JOE. He stumbles and fails miserably.

JOE. Ouch!

CORY. I'm sorry. I was trying to sweep you off your feet?

JOE. I got swept off my feet once today by Glen. I think that was enough. I really do need to hit the gym.

CORY. We'll hit the gym together.

JOE. It's a deal.

CORY. I'm warning you now, I'm no Richard Gere.

JOE smiles and takes his hand.

JOE. That's OK. I'm no Debra Winger.

They share a tender kiss and walk arm in arm out the French doors to join the party.

BLACKOUT
END OF PLAY

PROPERTY List

Wastebasket
Empty White Castle Sacks
French Fries
Trent's Gym Bag
Bag of Cat Food
Cup
Litter Box
Small Bag of Marijuana
Cat Carrier
Bette Davis DVD's
Over Night Bags
Road Map
Flashlight
Small Quilt
Can of Soda
Bag of Twizzlers
A Dollar Bill
Set of keys
Agnes's Walkie Talkie
PapersSmall Hand Towel
Joints
A Half Sheet of Drywall
Small Ax
Pillow and Blanket
Television Remote
Can of Pringles
Heather's Sketch Pad
Large Bag of Pork Rinds
Large Coil of Rope
Skinny Gazelle Sport Drinks
4 Clip boards with Papers and Pens
4 Kits w Clothes, Towels and Toiletries
4 Huge Books of Rules & Regulations

Glen's Yoga Mat
Printed Class Schedules
Swimmer's Mask
Life Jacket
Swimmer's Flippers
Four Crochet Hooks
Four Balls of Yarn
Four Crochet Projects
Cupcake with Candle
Bouquet of Flowers
Bottle of Wine
Small Bucket of Nails
Box of Chocolates
Small Birthday Balloon
Large Rubber Dildo
Large Picnic Basket
Bottle of Water
Registration Sheet
Patrick's Clip board with
Packs of Cigarettes /
Trent's School Books
Small Ladder
Donald's Whistle
Small Dead Insect
Agnes's Rolling Cart
Bottles of Liquor
Cigarette Lighters

Made in the USA
Monee, IL
01 April 2021